Cleaning House:

HOW TO GET YOUR KIDS BEGGING FOR CHORES

‘Go From Nagging To Bragging”

Shannon Scott Jensen

ISBN 10: 1492725838
ISBN 13: 9781492725831

TABLE OF CONTENTS

Video Trailer

www.cleaning-games.com/trailer

Dedication

This book owes its existence to my hero father and angel mother, Wayne and Ann Scott.

Publishers Notes

Disclaimer

The author and publisher specifically disclaim all responsibility for any liability, loss or risk, personal or otherwise, which is incurred as a consequence, directly or indirectly, from the use or application of any contents of this book.

Any and all product names referenced within this book are the trademarks of their respective owners. None of these owners have sponsored, authorized, endorsed, or approved this book.

Always read all information provided by the manufacturers' product labels before using their products. The author and publisher are not responsible for claims made by manufacturers.

About The Author

Shannon Jensen is a "kid in a grown-up person's skin" who still believes in the magic of imagination.

She earned her Bachelor's degree in Recreational Therapy and Youth Leadership from Brigham Young University. She was honored to receive a "Points of Light Award" from President George H.W. Bush" for developing "Handi-Capable Week" – a fun, popular program to teach how much those with disabilities are capable of.

She was a Recreational Therapist at the real "Hotel California" – a state Mental Hospital and Developmental Center where she worked with everyone from troubled gang teens to mentally ill seniors, and was given the "Woman of the Year" award.

She's served in numerous volunteer capacities including – chairing school events, participation on the PTA/PTO, as Scout leader, Special Olympics coordinator, church youth leader, camp director, missionary to Argentina, etc.

She's the oldest of six kids in a close-knit family.

Shannon's favorite roles are now wife and mother.

THANKS

. . . to the guy who doesn't expect any: my "FUN-derful" husband, **Kim Jensen**. Thanks for all the years of unselfish sacrifices to let me run around with a "butterfly net" chasing dreams. Any time I get to make a difference - it's you who should take the bow.

. . . to our beautiful daughter - **Jannine** who's helped me pilot test and refine the ideas found in this book through the years. Your own ideas are "da bomb!" What an amazing blessing to have you in our lives!

. . . to my editor, **Lorraine States**. You went so much farther than catching the goofs and getting me to ease up on all those dashes I love to throw in (Oh, yes! There were so many more before!). You are an artisan word-smith and I cherish every "dream-storm" we've cooked up and await your own book with much wringing of hands!

. . . to the idea lady herself - **Kim Meyers**! Stop being so modest! You really fueled my fire at the onset of this project with all the time you took to work through the concepts with me. I value your wise counsel, your out-of-the box thinking, and your smoothies!

. . . to **Carrie Scott**. Thanks so much for believing in this project enough ask to "suit up" and careen about the house setting things to "right" . . . and then setting things to "write" in your blog. Thanks for your contribution and the goofy pictures!

. . . to **Cathie Frost** who made time you didn't have to help bring that special brand of classy, that's always been yours, to this writing.

. . . to all of my "fun-tastic" friends who stepped up to help, for your Atlas-like support! You're the best!

MY GIFT TO YOU

Dear Reader!

I'm still new enough to authoring books, that I run and tell my family whenever a copy sells. So, thanks! It's a great honor that you'd buy this . . . and I'd like to "over-deliver" on your investment.

Here's a special link where you can get a free copy of my ebook ***"10 Unusual and Sometimes Funny Tips To Bring Fighting and Tantrums To a Screeching Halt."***

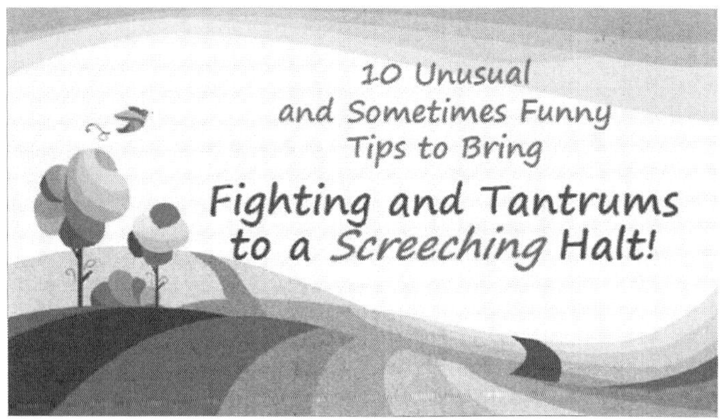

I'll be posting it for sale on Amazon.com but for now, I'd like to just give it to you. You can head on over to www.cleaning-games.com where you can request that a copy of the digital version be sent directly to you.

Again, thanks much!

Shannon

1 August 2013

PREFACE

The idea that we could actually have kids begging for chores seems absolutely impossible - even downright funny. What's the trick? Dangle a watch in front of them and tell them they're getting very sleepy? . . .

Is this a book about hypnosis and brainwashing our kids so that they'll look forward to helping out around the house? . . . Actually, it's the opposite.

The great Dale Carnegie once explained that to influence people, you need to address what they want and then show them how to get it. He went on to tell a story about Ralph Waldo Emerson and his son's efforts to get a calf into the barn.

He said, "They made the common mistake of thinking only of what they wanted: Emerson pushed and his son pulled, but the calf did just what they did: he thought only of what he wanted; so he stiffened his legs and stubbornly refused to leave the pasture."

Their Irish housemaid came to their rescue. " . . . she had more horse sense, or calf sense, than Emerson had. She thought of what the calf wanted; so she put her maternal finger in the calf's mouth, and let the calf suck her finger as she gently led him into the barn."

Now, with that in mind - imagine a slippery bar of soap in your wet hand. Squeeze tightly and the bar will pop out. Open your hand all the way and the bar will fall at the slightest tilt. Best way to hold that soap? -

Cradle it in your hand - in a comfortable balance.

You know where this is going, don't you?

If we as parents use too much pressure (like pushing the calf or squeezing the soap) on our children to get them to work - we foster resentment.

Neglect to give them responsibility - they fall into apathy.

No one really wins with either approach

And so - No.

This is not going to be a book about how to manipulate, trick or strong-arm our kids into getting their chores done.

"How To Get Your Kids Begging For Chores" is about helping us, the adults, to see from a kid's-eye view. It's about big-time leverage. It's about getting what we want by giving them what they want.

When you learn how to pull that off, you'll find that the "begging to do chores" will come, not because you've played mind games with your kids, but because they really, honestly enjoy helping out.

If that sounds like pure fiction, take heart!

It's already been done and you can do it too.

While our family is certainly not perfect - and our home don't always look like the cover of "Good Housekeeping" - still we have tested and continue to test the concepts you'll be reading about here. I can tell you with a content smile that the response has been great!

Let's let the kids speak for themselves:

"Bomb Squad helped us work faster and "funner" together as a family to get something done." **– Maddy age 13**

"I really liked it! It was better than doing work the normal way." **– Camille age 9**

"It was a fun, encouraging, and bond-building activity. The group building was my favorite part. It was a lot "funner" than doing chores by yourself." **- Bennett age 16**

"Bomb Squad was really fun. I really enjoyed it!" **– Nathan age 10**

"This is cool."
"Hurry, you're not cleaning!"
"Yes!" (When he stopped the bomb).
". . . we did that whole room in only10 minutes?!"
(My daughter said frantically) "What can I get?!"
"Hey! I want to dust!".

There was no complaining. I asked if they liked the game we played (not labeled cleaning), and they said, "Yes!"

- Sarah B. quoting her 9 year-old son, Jaden and 4 year-old daughter Aliyah during a cleaning adventure.

"I was having sooooooooooo much fun, I forgot I was working!" **– Jannine age 10**

. . . And what do parents think?

"It was great seeing my kids running around frantically cleaning the house!" – **Kim M.**

"It's the ultimate Oxymoron. Clean and fun shouldn't go together, but with this . . . it somehow works!" – **David J.**

Figuring out how to get my kids to do their chores has always been MY chore! We've tried charts, rewards and taking away privileges. This book gives me some new ideas to try to make it fun for ALL of us. Even if you try just one tactic, it's worth it!
– **"Busy Mom"** *(excerpt from Amazon.com review)*

This toy room was covered in toys and my nine-year-old, four-year-old and myself were able to clean it up in 10 minutes - including the toys hiding under the toy chest! – **Sarah B.**

" . . . my daughter has made a point of telling me when I am making chores fun and when I'm not. "You're not doing what the book says to make me beg for chores". My daughter has made it clear that she prefers positive ways to do chores rather than lectures about getting chores complete." – **Diane** *(excerpt from Amazon.com review)*

This book was great. Ever since I bought it, my kids have been doing chores every day. They do not complain! It's amazing! Susan "Mag-Reader" (excerpt from Amazon.com review)

In short - this book is about how to help both of you get what you want.

So, let's get to work . . .

CHAPTER 1: WINNING THE WAR . . . WITH A COOKBOOK

What would you say is the longest war ever waged?

The Roman-Persian wars?

The Vietnam War?

100-Year War between England and France? . . .

How about one that's been going on for likely over 7000 years? Its scope spans the continents. Its effect has been felt in every culture. Almost every person on earth has been affected by it in one way or another.

There are no generals. No lasting truces. And - in an ironic twist - the majority who have been on one side eventually switch ranks to join the other.

Which war is this that I'm sure you've already guessed?

The "Chore War!" - waged in the home between parents and their kids.

Of course, lives are not on the line in this war (although sometimes you wonder!) but it's a war just the same.

In one camp – kids are freedom fighters.
Their cause: Play.

In the other camp - parents champion responsibility. Their cause: Work.

Battles are played out through a host of tactics:

Stealth - ignoring, procrastinating and sneaking off.

Torture - whining, begging, lecturing and nagging.

Diversion - excuses, bribery and playing one parent against another.

Full Scale Assault - screaming, spanking, 'round-the-house chases and punishments.

It's an ongoing tug of war where one side has to lose ground for the other to win.

Certainly there are pockets of peace in homes where parents and kids see eye to eye . . . or one camp has simply surrendered to the other.

But this book is written for the rest of us: the majority who are tired - sick of fighting - and looking for a better way.

Surely the Yin-Yang of work and play - both good and needed - can coexist peacefully at the same time.

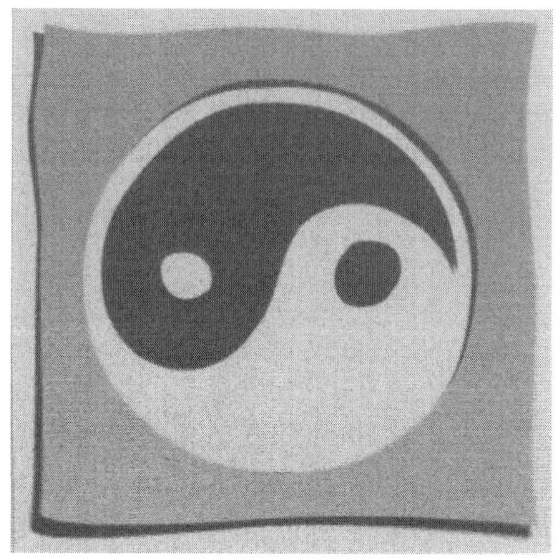

. . . Otherwise, this would be a very short book!

The good news: There absolutely is a way to break out the white flags and change the paradigm from battling to . . . baking . . . where everyone can have their cake and eat it too. Where work and play can "shake hands" and everyone wins!

Let's look at the most common recipe parents dish out when it's time to help.

It goes like this: Kids are given a job - or even a list of jobs and a deadline to get them done (usually - now).

That's the "Sawdust and Prunes" recipe.

It's distasteful for kids and popular with parents. Now, you can try to garnish it with a colorful "Work Wheel" or a shiny job chart, but in the end we're still dishing out marching orders.

I'll be honest. Even though I've written this book full of more tasteful recipes for work, "Sawdust and Prunes" is still on the menu at our house.

Although . . . we've cooked up a new way that's made it far more palatable for all of us.

Now, we start the day with a list of chores - but rather than tell our daughter Jannine which chore to get started on right away - I tell her that she has until "Whatever-o'-Clock" to complete any one of the tasks on her list and when to expect an inspection.

There is always more than enough time given. She chooses. There's no nagging. No excuses. Ahhhhhhh.

When each job is done, Jannine gets encouragement, my thanks and a new deadline until everything on the list is checked off.

If a chore isn't completed in the time given, then an extra job is simply added to the list as a consequence. If she completes an extra chore ahead of time - before the inspection - one of the remaining jobs on her list may be thrown out for the day.

For more "carrot and stick" motivation, I may say that she can go play with her friends, or get on the computer or do something else that rolls her socks up and down - once she's finished her list. Even this hasn't been necessary lately though.

Here's what Jannine has to say about it:

"It's not the most exciting thing, but I like it WAY better than before."

Even though she likes this way of serving it up, Sawdust and Prunes is not a recipe Jannine or any other sane kid will ever be begging for.

When it comes to chores - if you really want to have your cake and eat it too, you've got to change the recipe and add some new ingredients . . . starting with the proverbial "spoonful of sugar"

(Otherwise known as - FUN).

When you mix sweet fun to the flour of a job to be done, you're on your way to . . .

- ✓ Improving morale
- ✓ Giving a task a purpose that's new and meaningful to a kid
- ✓ Increasing productivity
- ✓ Fostering a sense of "team"
- ✓ Increasing loyalty to your family
- ✓ Speeding up the time it takes to clean up - sometimes dramatically
- ✓ Actually making "keeper" family memories

I don't think there needs to be a big sales job here.

Of course mixing fun into work would be great.

But how?

The good news is that you're holding an entire recipe book full of ideas that will turn plain, old chores into "activity treats" your kids will go after like seagulls to a shrimp boat!

You'll even learn how to cook up your own family favorites!

But before we get into these recipes - it's important to get to know what ingredients we'll be working with.

CHAPTER 2: THE D.N.A. OF F-U-N

So - What makes Fun . . . Fun?

Think about it this way:

D.N.A. (or deoxyribonucleic acid) has been called "The Blueprint of Life" It looks like a twisted ladder with 2 strands connected with 4 different types or rungs - or "bases" that can be combined in an infinite number of ways.

Each combination forms a unique genetic code found in every cell that determines how each living being will be made up. Blue eyes? Dark skin? Curly hair? The ability to do that "double-jointed-finger" thing? - Like Prego® sauce – "It's in there."

Fun has a similar "blueprint." At its core there are "building blocks" that can be combined in countless ways that determine how an activity will turn out. Each activity is unique.

Let's see how this works:

Imagine.

Your parents call your family together Saturday morning.

Time to get things done!

"Josh - please put on a pair of tights and stuff your shirt so you look like a cupcake with legs. Then - we want you to run back and forth outside for an hour while the neighbor kids knock you down repeatedly."

"Lulabelle - your job will be to sit in a chair and stare ahead without saying a word. Just wiggle your fingers and slide your arm around on the table."

"Okay, Sakiya - we want you to run about in wild circles, hopping and jumping about while people wave their hands in your face and try to steal from you."

Now - would you say Josh, Lulabelle, and Sakiya have somewhat weird - if not sadistic parents? . . . Or would you say they just told Josh to go play football, let Lulabelle get on FaceBook, and Sakiya is free to join her team for a game of basketball.

The reason those tasks didn't sound enjoyable at all is because I stripped away the "D.N.A. of F-U-N." Add these elements back, and you've got some of the top things kids love to do in their free time.

This then begs the question: "Is it possible to add this D.N.A. of F-U-N to any activity?"

Say . . . cleaning a bedroom . . . doing dishes . . . sorting laundry . . . pulling weeds . . . vacuuming . . . even changing a diaper?

The quick answer - it's already been done with many tasks that would otherwise be distasteful.

Sheep shearing for example - a hot, smelly, grimy job has been turned into an international sport, particularly popular . . . where they have sheep.

Since 1961, folks have come from all over the world to New Zealand for three days of fierce competition for the renowned "Golden Shears" event.

What about Spelling Bees? Who would have believed that young children would take to reading and even memorizing the dictionary? Even sand doesn't get that dry!

But someone made it a demanding competition - and kids are lining up!

Racing about a hot kitchen trying to come up with a gourmet meal, on a tight schedule, for very finicky folks should induce ulcers galore - instead, it's become the TV hits "Iron Chef" and "Chopped" - and not only do top chefs line up to cook under these conditions - people actually watch them even though they can't even smell the food, let alone taste it.

I can even tell you that years ago, as a family camp counselor, the other staffers and I turned the drudgery of diaper changing - sometimes for up to 25 infants - into a spirited Pamper-Off.

The babies certainly had fun! . . . And if memory serves . . . I just know I won every time!

And "Competition" is just one building block in the D.N.A. of F-U-N.

Here's list of more at your disposal:

CHALLENGE

IMAGINATION

RULES OF THE GAME

REWARDS & PENALTIES

MEASURABILITY

EMPOWERMENT & STRATEGY

THE EXTRAORDINARY

EXCITEMENT

SOCIALIZATION

PROPS

HUMOR & PLAYFULNESS

There are likely more, and I'd love to hear from you if you think of them, but for now - these will be building blocks that make up the D.N.A. of F-U-N that we're going to get into in a minute.

But first, let's look at the flip side: What makes Work . . . Work? It's any activity that's either partially or fully devoid of those building blocks listed above.

It's the "have to do's" vs. the "want to do's."

It's the attitude you have toward whatever motions you're going through – not the actual task.

Now, to tie this into the idea of going from "battling" to "baking" - let's imagine separating these building blocks of F-U-N and dropping each into its own colorful jar. Let's then take these glowing jars . . . and label each bottle as an Ingredient of FUN.

Let's put these jars into a cupboard that we'll call "The Pantry of Fun."

CHAPTER 3: THE PANTRY OF FUN

The same way a good chef understands the subtleties of each spice . . . or the way an onion will "give itself up" to peanut butter pâté . . . or the "personality" of a breadstick brought out when it's dipped in yak milk . . .

the more we understand each ingredient of FUN the more artistic we can become when we're dishing out chores.

Of course, you'll rarely use - all or even most - ingredients in your recipes.

Many times, just one or two will do the trick.

So, let's open up these jars and get to understand what's inside each a little better.

Challenge is one of the most heavily used jars in the Pantry of Fun. It's easy to come up with challenges. They give us a chance to see how well we measure up - and to enjoy a feeling of success when we come out on top. Ultimately - we get to learn something about ourselves.

It may take the form of competition . . . beating your "personal best" score . . . time limits . . . obstacles . . . brain teasers . . . a rite of passage . . . the works! Whatever form it takes - challenge is an art form. Too much - and you risk being overwhelmed. Too little - and the challenge becomes at best - boring and at worst - insulting.

So, balance is the trick.

Perhaps the most addictive challenges are the short, bite-sized ones. It's like eating Doritos® chips - you start with just one and pretty soon, you've chowed-down on the whole bag with the "just one more" mentality.

Computer games and Casinos in particular have cashed in on these "morsel challenges." If you fail - hey! . . . you can always go back for a "do-over" and with a little course correction, in no time you'll surely be on your way to the top.

Challenge is also one of the easiest ingredients to add to housework. Here's a few ideas to get you started . . .

Beat Your Family

Turn on a timer when you're taking on a chore. See who can beat the record, even if it's your own.

Ad Dash

Before watching TV - hand out 3x5 cards with bite-sized tasks on them that should take no longer than 5 minutes. (Throwing in a load of laundry . . . cleaning out the kitty litter box . . . loading the dishwasher . . . taking out the trash . . . burglar-proofing your home with concrete . . .). Now, when the commercials hit, everyone jumps up and runs to get their task done before the show comes back on.

Early-Bird Racers

Post all chores that need to be done first thing in the morning along with the number of chores each child is expected to do. Then - 'first come-first served! The child who gets started early can pick from any chore on the list. Those who dawdle along will get the leftover jobs no one else wanted.

Kids can only select one task at a time, so someone can't come at the beginning of the day, pick all the good jobs and then sit on them.

Parents can get in on this too – especially if there's only one child in the family. Of course, there also may need to be some allowances if you have a big age gap. For example – a 4 year old may be willing, but changing the oil on the car could be a little unfair to ask.

Whenever you can, try to throw in especially enjoyable jobs – like washing the car or painting a dresser or making dinner. If all chores are about the same, there won't be a lot of motivation to 'hustle those bustles!"

The House Cup

You can make your own House Cup. Hit the thrift stores where there's always trophies to be found . . . or splurge and buy a new one. Along with that - set up a sheet that will track who won the house cup when and mount it somewhere for all to see.

You may choose to include prizes that go with the cup (a trip to the movies . . . ice cream . . . a toy . . . whatever motivates!)

Divide up into teams. Could be kids vs. parents . . . boys vs. girls . . . random drawing . . . or everyone for themselves!

Teams can earn extra points for helpfulness, team spirit and extra-mile acts of kindness. They can lose points for the opposite.

Award the Cup in a simple weekly ceremony - and if you really want to ramp it up - throw in some goodies and games and invite the neighbors for the presentation.

If you only have one kid in your family or you want to expand the challenge, consider inviting friends and neighbors to join in the competition at their own homes - just make sure all adults are on the same page when it comes to dishing out points.

4. **The Sorting Basket**

You'll see it show up several times in this book. It's a fast way to round up and corral a mess. You can instantly clean a room, by just throwing everything into the Sorting Basket.

There is one hitch that our family ran into with this - I was leaving the Sorting Basket on the floor in our daughter Jannine's closet where she could get into it anytime she wanted. So, when she wanted something, she'd rummage through the basket - throwing everything else back on the floor.

We solved this by putting the basket out of reach, except once each evening. Then, like the phantom ship "The Flying Dutchman" or the lost city of Glocca Morra, the Sorting Basket would appear - but only for a short period. It was just long enough for her to get what she wanted out of it - and everything she took out had to be put where it belonged.

The Sorting Basket challenge can be worked several ways:

- You could do a time challenge. See how many things can be pulled from the basket and put away in - say 10 minutes - before the basket disappears again. (Tip:

Count out the items to be put away before starting the clock)

- Or . . . this could be done as a competition challenge . See who can put everything away first.
- Or you can do a combination: Who can put the most items away in 10 minutes?

Loco Garden

See how many weeds you can pull in the garden - blindfolded! (kidding . . . kidding . . .)

The bottom line here is that almost all chores are a challenge. The trick is to make each an interesting one.

Imagination

Which do you think would be more interesting?

The toy car you push across the floor few times, or

. . . a car that can fly, dive under water (hopefully with the windows up!) and blast sonic waves at a Pterodactyl belonging to Dr. Sludge, the dark raider, who is chasing you because you're carrying the microchip in this car that has the only existing plans to a device that can turn bubble gum off the sidewalk into hot dogs!?

The second could easily be the very same car as the first with a dash of imagination sprinkled on top.

Imagination can transport you and your kids to another world, endow superpowers, present thrilling challenges, and bring magic to anything.

Does that "anything" include work? Let's see . . .

- Ever read the sparkly children's series "Mrs. Piggle Wiggle?"

  Her cure for one girl who wouldn't clean up was for both of them to imagine that they'd been captured by a witch and forced to work for her so they had to ready the house before the witch returned.

Once the house was clean, Mrs. Piggle Wiggle left the room to keep a lookout and returned dressed as the witch (blanket overhead like a crone's shawl) for a "frightening" inspection.

- Richard and Linda Eyre in their book "Three Steps To A Strong Family" fixed up a large sack to look like a wide-mouthed "monster" that would come around in the evening and "eat" anything the kids hadn't put away. Kids could "rescue" the items by doing extra chores later.

- Imagine you're hosting a TV show and demonstrating the right way to tidy up a house. Talk to an imaginary audience as you demonstrate your prowess.

  In fact - why not turn on the video camera for real and take turns filming your show? If you know some basic editing - you could even throw in fun effects like high speed and slow-motion. Just be playful with the camera. Break out the popcorn and watch later.

- Pretend you're part of a stealth strike force that picks a target (say a bathroom . . . bedroom . . . dishes) that's been overtaken and trashed by the enemy. Your mission: Rescue and Restore before sunset - without getting caught. You must be sneaky and avoid observation at all cost. Missions could even be handed out on official looking cards.

What "Play-Dreams" can you concoct?

- Is that a dishwasher - or a hungry pet dinosaur?
- Are those weeds - or food supplies you're gathering to survive on a deserted island?
- Are you mopping the kitchen floor - or swabbing the deck of a pirate ship while you spy on the captain to recover a stolen treasure map?
- Are you vacuuming or is that a metal detector to help you find that treasure?
- Are you just taking out the garbage, or are you disguised as the janitor to help free your friend who's hiding in there after being shrunk at a secret lab?

There's someone who came up with the term "Chore War" long before I did. In fact, they've got a website dedicated to the term. ChoreWars.com does a great job using imagination to turn household tasks into a role playing game. Here's a humorous video that gives a quick overview: http://youtu.be/4kczm-iJsGo

The idea is that you get to pick a fantasy character that gets to go on adventures. The more chores you do, the more experience points (XP) you get to help you grow in strength and skills in your fight against monsters and a quest for treasures.

Your character can join a team of other characters (other family members and friends from anywhere). It also lets you compete with people from all over the world. It's geared to older kids and even parents.

This is a free service and I think it could use more marketing, but others who have been using it, are very enthusiastic about it. Don't miss the opening picture like I did. Each character has something unexpected in their hands (Jannine had to point th is out to me).

I'll have more about this service on the blog section of our site once we've had a chance to "kick the tires" a bit. You can check it out yourself at www.chorewars.com .

Rules of the Game

I once taught an early-morning, youth, church class before school. One day, the kids arrived to find a colorful game (The Omega Virus) laid out before them.

It had robots and astronauts. There was a talking, control panel where you could hear the voices of an evil computer virus with an attitude and a the ship's computer crying out for help. There were folding sectors that could be closed down and backpacks full of gizmos and gadgets. In short - it was cool!

Of course, the class swooped in for a better look. I invited them to go for it.

"But what do we do?" one asked.

"Just play!" I urged.

They flipped switches, moved pieces about, pushed buttons . . . exploring . . . for less than 5 minutes. Finally, one young man blurted, "This is STUPID!"

Perfect.

The teaching moment had arrived.

"What's wrong?" I asked. "This is a fun game."

"But, we don't know the rules," said another.

"Aren't rules restrictive? Boring? I queried. "Can't you just have fun?"

By then, they knew where I was going - and I went there. I asked something like this:

"What if Michael Jordan (this was in the pre "Yao Ming" days) decided to just hike the ball under his arm and run down the court without dribbling? What would the fans scream? How fun would the game be? Whose team would win?

"Or how about this? - Bernice buys a cell phone and reads the instructions about plugging it in when the battery runs low - but she doesn't want to be bothered with pesky little things like the laws of physics.

"How would you like to be operated on by a surgeon who cheated his way through medical school to impress his girlfriend?"

We went on to have a great discussion about how understanding and accepting good laws and rules make life better - even more fun. In fact, I'd recommend this as an object lesson you can do with your own kids. Any fun-looking board game will do.

The rules of housekeeping work the same way. And the better the rules, the better your chance of enjoying even chores!

Sure, parents set rules like "You can't use the X-Box until you've picked up all the junk on the floor in your room. That's clearly a "Sawdust and Prunes" recipe.

But what if you added to the rules?

" . . . and the Sorting Basket must be placed on a table and you can come no closer to it than this line to throw in your stuff." You've just used rules to mix in challenge.

You can make it even more interesting by sprinkling in competition, like this:

"Divide the room. You and your opponent pick sides and cannot cross the line. Your sorting baskets are placed on the opposite side of the line – your opponent's side. The object of the game is to fill your basket with as many items as you can in 10 minutes. If you miss your basket, your opponent captures that item and may throw it into their basket.

Now - how about pulling out another jar from the Pantry and adding a dash of imagination to the rules:

"You are imprisoned by the Omygolly Tribe and must escape their Room-Doom Pit.

The winners of each challenge - may claim the Orb for that level (a ball wrapped in aluminum foil with a point value written on it - say from 5 to 20). The Orbs are larger with each level. The bigger the Orb - the more valuable.

Once a player has completed each level, they will be 'dropped a ladder' (not a real one - we're just pretending, of course.) to advance to the next level of the Pit (another room in the house) to face the next challenge.

You can have a different challenge in each room:

It may simply be more difficult: "On this next level - the baskets will be smaller, higher and farther apart . . ."

Or you may imagine something completely different: "This room is filled with lava. Only those who are able to clean their side first without touching the floor will escape with the orb."

Then mix in a REWARD so each player has something to work toward: "Prizes, glory and/or snacks await those who can make it to the top of the pit."

The winner(s) with the most Orb points becomes chief of the tribe for the day.

(You can make a great "chief" hat with aluminum foil, feathers, stickers – whatever – and "crown" the winner). All the other players will do their best teeka lacka pooka dance around the chief in celebration!

Now – this is just an example. You can pick and choose any rules you want. You can also decide how many rooms ("levels") will you have. Feel free to design this - or any other activity rules to fit your family's ages, interest, number of members, and so on.

The point here is that rules can make chores far more interesting - especially when you throw in other ingredients from the Pantry of Fun.

Now, you may ask, "Won't too many rules make cleaning complicated?" It's really up to you - and if you want to stick with simple rules, it's your call.

But if you and your kids do want to ramp up the rules - here's one take away thought : Our Trivial Pursuit game says (So it must be true!) that Football is the sport with the most rules . . . and yet . . . it's also one of the most popular games out there.

Bottom line: You are the best to judge what works for your family.

Rewards & Penalties

REWARDS

Here's a story to share with your kids:

There was once a princess who owned a beautiful crown. And the very best part of that crown was the massive and brilliant jewel set in the center.

One day, while she played at the park, she realized that her crown was lighter. She reached up and - the jewel was gone.

She and her servants scoured the park for the rest of the day - searching. But, they returned to the castle that night dejected.

The next day, the princess issued a proclamation to all the kingdom.

It read:

"WHOSO FINDETH THE ROYAL JEWEL

WITHIN 30 DAYS TIME

SHALL BE GIVEN A PALACE OF THEIR OWN

AND NEVER KNOW WANT AGAIN.

. . . BUT . . .

IF 30 DAYS HATH PASSED

AND ONE IS DISCOVERED POSSESSING THE JEWEL

– THAT PERSON WILL BE

SENTENCED TO DEATH."

Not long after the proclamation went out, a young man was in the park with his dog. The dog spotted a chipmunk and chased it under a bush. When the dog emerged, he had in his mouth - you guessed it! - The jewel.

The young man examined it, thought for a few minutes and . . . took it home, where he hid it under a bed until the 30 days had gone by.

Then, he went to the palace and knocked on the door.

"I would like to see the princess," he said.

"The princess is busy," the guards said.

"It's about the jewel."

"Oh! The princess will see you now."

He was lead into the throne room where sat a very depressed princess.

"Your highness, I believe this is yours," said the young man, producing the jewel.

The princess gasped. "Where did you find it?"

"In the park."

"When did you find it?" said she.

"A few days after you lost it," said he.

"Don't you realize that if you had brought this back yesterday, I could have rewarded you beyond your dearest dreams?" asked the princess.

"Yes, indeed," the young man replied. "I read the proclamation."

"But then, you must also know that now, I can have you killed! Why, oh why did you wait until today?!" asked a now utterly confused princess.

"Your majesty - when I found the jewel I thought to myself, 'Self - will you bring this back because you want something?' A reward did not seem like a good reason to return something that wasn't mine. 'Well, will I bring it back because I'm afraid not to?' Fear did not seem a good reason either. So - I waited to bring it back today simply because it was the right thing to do."

NOTE: The princess did not have him killed. Instead, they ended up getting married, were well loved by all in the kingdom . . . and the dog got his own rodent ranch.

Now, wouldn't it be great to help our kids get past the point of helping out to get a reward or to avoid a penalty?! To do - simply because it's "the right thing to do." We all want our kids to discover that the value of work and the satisfaction of a job well done is a gift you give to yourself as much as others. "Good things comes to thems that serves!"

But, I'll be the first to agree that often, you need a bridge that will help kids cross over to this mature understanding of work. Rewards and penalties can serve as that bridge.

Most games tie rewards and penalties into the rules like a contract:

'Do this - get this.' There's a consistency that can be counted on.

Rewards may be money, gifts, medals, getting their initials posted on a list of winners, points, or a little mustachioed cartoon guy jumping up and down, saying, "So nice!"

This is a very valid system that works on so many levels. You wouldn't want to score a home run that clears all the bases and then have the umpire say, "Well . . . okay. You did bring in four runners, but I'm only going to give you two points."

Nor would you want to work all week at your job and be told by your boss, "Yeeeeessss - you did everything I asked you to do, but I just don't feel like paying you this time around.

Maybe next week . . ."

However, there are times when consistent rewards can be a problem. They can lead to unrealistic expectations and those expectations lead to demanding (read "spoiled") behavior.

Yesterday, our vacationing family visited the Rock of Gibraltar. At the top were signs everywhere - big fines for anyone caught feeding the Barbary Apes that ran free up there.

That didn't stop a group of laughing young men from tossing a candy bar to a particularly large and scruffy primate matriarch. Of course, you know that animals who develop a taste for people food will become more and more aggressive to get it again - putting even small kids at risk.

Concerned - I squared off with the "Big Mama" - trying to get back the bar while calling for the staff, who were nowhere to be found. I chased her - hoping she'd drop the treat. But she leapt to the wall and barred her teeth at me. We were about a foot apart. She held the bar aloft and looked at me with an expression that clearly said, "Your move, Turkey!"

. . . And it was I who backed down - not wanting to find out how serious she was. I found out later that day the easy way. I just asked.

"Someone is bitten here just about every day," said our cable car guy. "Yesterday, we sent someone to the hospital." If they know you have food, they don't wait for you to give it. They'll take it any way they can."

Sound familiar? Know anybody like that - bitten by the "I'm entitled" bug? Want to avoid reward overdose with your kids? Me too.

So what if we all went to the other extreme? No rewards.

Are you ready to deal with the disappointment when your child comes to you and reports that they've mowed the lawn, changed the baby's diaper, and set up a Ham Radio for emergencies - and all you can say is, "That's nice - but I've got nothing for you, kid."

How do you teach and motivate your kids to work without any incentives?

Fortunately - getting kids to help out isn't an all or nothing deal.

The answer lies in random - often unexpected - rewards.

So! Just when you thought it was safe to sit down - here's another "run-in-with-royalty" story!

Long ago, a great king had a mighty road built that spanned one end of the kingdom to the other. The king decided to open it to the people with a great event - a contest.

The one who could travel the King's Highway the best would be rewarded with a fortune in gold.

The day of the contest arrived and with it - half the kingdom.

Many came in their finest of clothes and draped in jewels. Others came upon sleek and muscular steeds, pulling the most modern of coaches. Some had trained for weeks, to run like a mountain stream in the spring. They were dressed in lightweight clothing and sturdy shoes.

A large gong was struck and everyone began to move. All through the day, each traveled the King's Highway in the manner they thought best.

Towards evening, the runners and fancy-pants coaches arrived - racing to cross the end of the road first. They were followed by the rich and refined who cared little for speed - but for show. As they passed before the king, they gestured grandly as servants blew upon trumpets and waved large fans for an unforgettable parade of finery.

Each participant marveled at the wonder that was the great road, with its well-crafted bridges, straight lines cut through the hills and the inviting trees that cooled the way.

And everyone - not to complain of course - "reported" that there was only one mistake the builders had made: Just after the only sharp bend in the road, a large pile of rocks had been heaped on it and forgotten.

What a time each had trying to get around it!

The sun set and almost everyone had returned home. But the king remained to watch and wait. There was one subject who had not yet returned.

Finally! . . . a dark shape emerged on the road. An old mother. Her hair was disheveled, her clothes torn in several places - and she was filthy! She was also dragging a large sack behind her as she stopped before the king.

"Sire," she said, bowing. "I am sorry to have kept you waiting so long."

"Why have you arrived so late and so very dirty?" questioned the king.

"King, I must report to you that there was a pile of rocks on the road . . . I feared someone might not see it in time and be hurt. I moved it away and found this at the bottom of the pile." - And she held out the heavy sack.

"I cannot explain how it came to be there, but someone has lost this gold. Would you help me find the owner?"

"I can . . . and I have," replied the king. "The one who travels the road best - is the one who leaves it better. The gold is yours."

My dad understood this principle. He'd been after us kids to change the toilet paper tube when it ran out - and we just had it in our heads that someone else would do it, so we never bothered.

One day - I don't know what possessed me - but I changed a spent tube. Inside, I found a crisp $1 bill that had been waiting for the first child to listen to Dad. Now, it wasn't a deed to a palace in there, but do you think we were into changing toilet paper tubes after that?

It became a national pastime at our home!

Brainstorming: Here are a few ways you might "booby trap" your home with random rewards:

Leave a coupon for a small prize or a little bonus money

. . . taped to a plate in a dishwasher full of clean dishes

. . . in a sock in a pile of laundry that needs sorting.

. . . fastened to the handle of a garbage can.

You can mix it up to keep them guessing - just make sure you put a surprise in the same place more than once so they'll return to that task again and again in the hopes that another treat might await. Be clear, of course, that the reward can be claimed only when the job is done - it's easy to enforce if you use coupons that need to be redeemed.

The Tooth Fairy. Santa Claus. Barney.

Consider adding one more mythical creature to your family folklore: **Waydago** (read "Way To Go") the elf from the land of Thumbsup.

Waydago is an unpredictable, sneaky elf with extremely large eyes that never miss a thing. He's also got very big thumbs. He loves to stick them up, wave them in the air and do a little dance when he sees a kid doing great things! The problem is that he's always getting those thumbs stuck in doors (if you hear sounds in the night - it's just Waydago bumbling around).

He loves to spy and sneak up on unsuspecting kids that have done a worthy deed and hide a tiny, happy message - sometimes with a little gift - in odd places around the house - say in the fridge, a cereal box, or an umbrella.

One fun way to leave a Waydago message (perhaps occasionally with instructions of where to find a little, hidden, thank you treat) is to write a bitty-little note, on a small, colorful strip of paper and roll it into a tiny tube. Cut a colorful straw into ½ inch segments. (They look like teeny-weeny, colorful napkin holders!) Slide one of these 1/2 inch straws over the note and you've got a scroll from Waydago!

The more specific the message - pointing out each act of kindness - the more unique and appreciated each note will be.

High 5 Tickets are a way you can reward your kids randomly by giving them a numbered ticket and putting their name on it when they do something positive (chores on time . . . helping out a sibling . . . coming immediately when called . . . taking care of a responsibility without being asked . . . winning the Nobel Peace Prize . . . whatever positive behavior you want to reinforce.

All tickets go into a jar where weekly they, will be drawn for prizes (could be "Get Out Of Chore" free passes, an all-expense paid breakfast date with a parent, a goldfish bowl, a slumber party for up to 5 guests . . . wherever your imagination takes you and whatever motivates your kids.

Of course, the more tickets, the better the chances of winning. You can choose to award more than one prize at a drawing, letting kids pick their prizes in the order their tickets are drawn until every child has had a chance to pick a prize. In this case, the one with the most tickets is the one most likely to be drawn early on.

Penalties

Penalties can also serve a useful purpose in making work more enjoyable.

Whoa! Did I just say that?!

This idea is understandably harder for parents (me too) to employ because, penalties obviously don't sound fun at all.

But penalties and rewards are flip sides of the same coin. A good penalty will not belittle or discourage a player. Instead - penalties give realistic feedback and a reason to stretch. They make the game interesting - even exciting in a way that can ramp up the adrenaline in an effort to avoid them.

Penalties, administered correctly are a perfectly acceptable part of a kid's world. They expect that when the ball goes out of bounds - the other team gets it . . . when the Knight takes the Queen - she comes off the chessboard . . . and that when you drive your car into the wall too many times in a video game - it's going to roll over and blow up.

The older a kid grows, the less they expect to hear, "Well - you were tagged - but you don't have to be "It." or "No you didn't win that race, but we're going to give all of you a medal anyway." or "Hey - you don't seem to have nearly as much Monopoly money as your sister - let's just grab a handful of cash from the bank for you."

How boring! What would be the point of trying if you're just going to have the reward handed to you anyway?! By giving too much, we risk robbing our kids of a real sense of achievement when they do succeed.

The trick to make the *penalty itself* fun.

Nickelodeon "slimed" kids who didn't answer enough questions correctly - dumping a large bucket of rubbery, blubbery slime on a player.

The hit game show "Still Standing" had a trapdoor under each player and if they guessed wrong, they would drop out of sight (hopefully, onto a very large and plump pillow . . . or at least a stage-hand!).

Our 5th grade teacher, Mr. Tony - used to make kids wear their gum on their nose if he caught them chewing it in class.

So! - How do penalties look when you're cleaning and trying to be fun?

Here's a few ideas to get you wringing your hands with an evil chuckle of anticipation . . .

- Why not hit the thrift store with your kids and pick out the goofiest clothes - starting in the hat section - you can find. Now, if a job isn't done by its deadline, the penalty could be: Wear one of the goofy items – and keep adding funny clothes for each deadline missed. This could go in reverse too – remove a silly item each time a task is completed well.

- Try playing a favorite game to determine who does what chore. For example, you break out a pack of Uno cards. The stakes: who gets to wash the car and who gets to wash the toilet. The winner gets to pick which chore they want and the one who didn't win gets what's left. (Personally - I'd go for the toilet! Yes, it's gross, but it's easier and faster.)

- Take on one of the winner's chores for the day. Say - Sarah had her room cleaned by the stroke of noon while Oglethorpe laid around reading comics instead of getting things done. Sarah was supposed to clean the kitty litter box - but now she gets to give the job to Oglethorpe.

- Another penalty might simply be to do a funny stunt. The best ones will be the ones the kids come up with themselves.

  One example would be to sing a song of the winner's choosing, while standing in the bathtub (after all – it even comes with stage curtains and it's the place with the best acoustics in the house!). - And I don't need to explain that this is fully clothed - right? :o)

- Fill a bucket with wadded up newspaper balls or clean-rolled up socks - and drop them (from a chair, ladder, balcony . . .) onto the head of the penalized one.

- Get "creamed" - sprayed with whipped or shaving cream (outside or in the shower is best)

- Have a "Sock Midway" penalty - where the penalized person moves back and forth 10 times (think shooting gallery ducks) while the winner gets to throw 10 rolled up socks (preferably clean) at the "duck."

It's a good idea to make sure all are in agreement about what the penalty will be before taking on a challenge so you're not imposing something that could be humiliating for someone who wasn't prepared to have that penalty in the first place.

You might be thinking – if these penalties are too fun, my kids will do the wrong thing just to get one. In that case, you can reverse the rule and say that the ones who make the right choices get to choose their consequences. For those who didn't perform – parents choose the consequence. You know your kids and you're the final word.

Now, I'll be honest here - coming up with penalties while keeping the spirit of good cleaning fun is a trick. So, if you've got any feedback or new ideas for penalties, I'd love to hear your thoughts! Please visit our forum page (www.cleaning-games.com/forum) and go to "Fun Penalties."

Now you may say, "That's all well and good, but what I really need is an ongoing game where the penalties are on autopilot . . . where I don't have to be "the bad guy" all the time . . . and where there are no hard feelings."

Well – okay – you've talked me into it. I've got that game for you. We just came up with it recently and it's been hugely successful.

Hostage:
The rules are simple. Whenever someone drops something in a place where it's not supposed to be and leaves it there for more than 30 minutes, it becomes vulnerable. Any family member may then take that item hostage and store it away in a secure place (a drawer, a cupboard, sack . . .).

The only way to get that item that's now being held, is to hold a hostage negotiation. Family members may do a direct trade –

one hostage for another, or something especially valuable for several less important items.

If someone doesn't have any hostages to trade, then they can negotiate for a ransom. A ransom can be anything – a back-scratch, a treat, the remote control to the TV for the evening, taking over a chore, loaning a favorite toy . . . whatever has value to the kidnapper.

At our home, we've set up safe zones, like the bedrooms and Dad's office, where hostages cannot be taken. We'll also do a hostage negotiation whenever one is called for.

You may decide to ramp it up and say there can only be one per day or even week. The harder you make it for someone to recover their items the greater the chance of generating frustration which may be a real wake up call for hard-cases and the call is yours to make.

On the other hand - if something is taken hostage and there is no real effort to get it back, then it may be time to talk about giving it to another family member or even to charity.

This game flat out works!

Knowing that there's a real chance that something you've put down will not be waiting there for you when you return for it, or that another family member is scoring more hostages than you are, or that it's going to take more time delivering a ransom than it would to just put something away in the first place really motivates everyone to take those few extra steps to put that stuff where it's supposed to go!

Measurability

Could you imagine the Olympics without measurement?

What if the judge were to say, "Just begin whenever you feel the time is right for you. There isn't really a starting line. You just start where you'd like and run on over there until you're tired, because there's no finish line either."

What if there was no bar to clear or measuring tape for the pole vault or broad jump. Say judges didn't award points, but simply clapped or frowned at the figure skating competition?

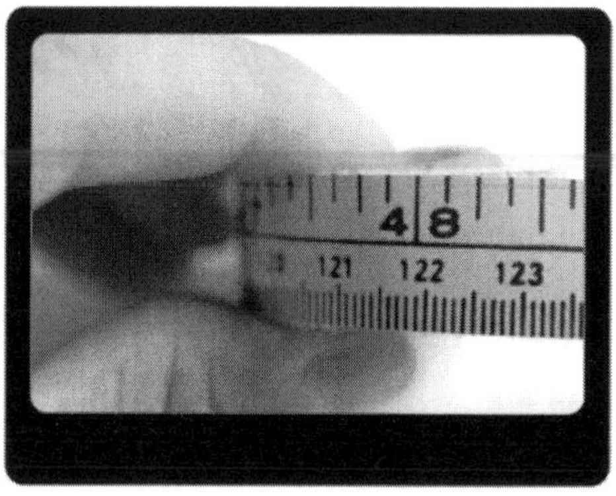

What if no one knew who held the world's record in each event because no one kept track?

What if there were no gold, silver and bronze medals to be won?

What if the boundary lines were erased for the volleyball championships?

Would the world gather round to watch such an event?

Measurement lets you see exactly how you've done and adds definition to your task. Being judged or being able to judge yourself gives substance to praise and clarity to constructive criticism.

When Jannine was smaller and words didn't mean much to her - I introduced the "Room-Mom-Meter" It was a long, thin candy box. I looped a ribbon from the top to bottom and fastened an arrow to it, to make a thermometer of sorts.

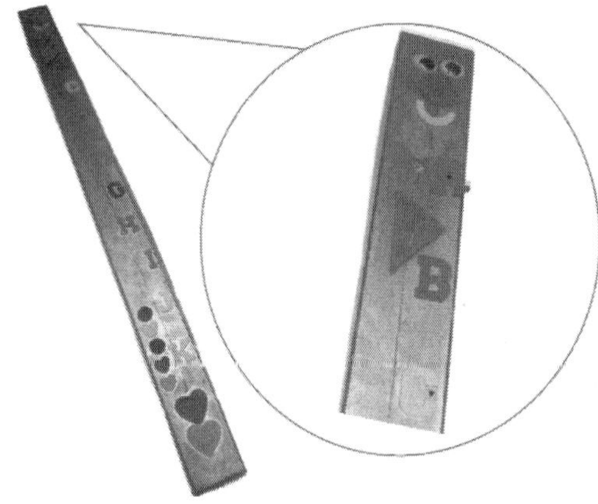

I let Jannine decorate it. She used letters – with "A" at the top. You could also just have more smiley-faces, stars and stuff the higher you go.

When it was time to clean her room I'd wave the "Room-Mom-Meter" about the room as if doing a sensor sweep and make electronic sound effects (deeee-ga, deeee-ga, deeee-ga)

Then, I'd slide the ribbon up or down depending on the current condition of the room until the ribbon gave the read-out. If the arrow was down toward the bottom, there was work to do.

Then I'd hang it on the wall, so Jannine could clearly see how her room measured up in her baseline score.

Then, she'd get to work cleaning and called me when she was ready for a new readout.

She loved watching the arrow climb - indicating a job very well done and would laugh when it would bump the top and strain to go higher. It was tangible praise.

I'd measured cleanliness.

There plenty of ways to do it.

You can pick up free stats charts from the "Toolbox" portion of our website if you'd like to track your fastest times for loading/unloading a dishwasher, vacuuming, cleaning a bathroom - whatever! These measurements can also take in competition (siblings vs. siblings or parents vs. kids) or you could let each kid focus on improving their own scores.

Speed is an easy thing to track, but can you measure style?

The popular show "Dancing With The Stars" does it all the time. Teams will twirl and swoop and glitter and slide the night away. Each doing a different routine to different music. It's the judges' job to boil down all the elements into a number to wave on a card in the air.

It's their "thermometer" readout.

Is it an accurate, objective number? Nope! The judges often hold up different numbers that can reflect everything from their personal opinions to their mood to whether they ate something that didn't agree them.

But those numbers mean everything to the dancers and fans because they're a tangible measurement from a credible source.

The show "Iron Chef" judges the creativity and skills of chefs, by giving specific ingredients - often pretty weird ones - and a meal category. Then, they turn on the timer.

So, for example - "Today, we have cream and sardines. Your task is to make a desert. You have 20 minutes. The clock starts now!" Chefs run about a fully equipped kitchen, using whatever tools and ingredients they'd like - to come up with the tastiest dish.

When the time is up, judges will tell each chef what worked and what didn't with each dish.

Now, I've been playing with this concept. How could you do something similar with tasks in the home?

One simple approach: When it comes time to make dinner, why not try an "Iron Chef Cook-Off - Homestyle Edition!"? Family members could be given a set of weird ingredients and each night one member or team would get their turn to make a meal using those ingredients. You may want to invite friends over to be your impartial judges (and they get a free meal out of the deal!)

Or, how about expanding this beyond the kitchen?

Divide the yard up into sections (one for each person or team participating). You could use gardening or landscaping as the category. Make sure you get a "before" picture!

Each team is then given their ingredients - say - a pallet of flowers, a string of Christmas lights, and a basket.

Each team gets one hour (or longer if you'd like) to incorporate their "ingredients" into the most amazing, extreme yard transformation they can come up with - using any tools from the garage they'd like.

In this example, it might be fun to run this competition towards evening so the string of lights will look their best. Remember to take "After" pictures. If it's possible to print both - all the better!

While the judges judge - competitors can grab a shower and return for a picnic . . . and the judges verdict.

You can have more than one award if you'd like:

- Most creative
- Most Whimsical
- Biggest change
- Most likely to be featured on the cover of "Better Homes and Gardens."
- Most likely landing site for a UFO . . .?!!!

This approach could also be used on a smaller scare about the house. You can switch landscaping "ingredients" with anything else that suits your fancy. These changes don't have to be permanent, but you might like them enough to leave them up a few days:

Here's a few categories and "ingredients" to give you a flavor :

Bathrooms: Stuffed animals, a flower and a beach towel

Family Room (divided up): A scrapbook, artwork from school and a roll of toilet paper.

Bedrooms: A fun noodle, lamp and umbrella

Kitchen: Small lanterns on a string, A bag of "puffballs," and a watering can.

This is an exercise in creative expression and the focus should be on fun and making memories. Parents would make obvious judges, but siblings and friends could fill the role too. In fact you could even post pictures of entries on FaceBook and invite everyone to vote!

If you've got neighbors you think would enjoy this kind of competition, consider expanding the "playing ground" to include their homes and yards.

Another way to measure is a point system that leads to that "House Cup" I mentioned earlier. You can make one from scratch or hit the thrift store to find an old trophy. Use tin foil to add your own embellishments. For example, you might make teeny, tiny paint brushes, brooms . . . even a little lawn mower if you're ambitious!

Whenever a task has been performed well or an attitude has been especially cheerful . . . and act of kindness rendered unexpectedly - award points.

Performance can be measured using time limits, boundaries, photography, points, ranking, statistics, etc.

Points can also be taken away for negative behavior.

Then once a month (or however often works best for you), one approach would be to dress up and hold a special family dinner in honor of the winner of the House Cup. Reveal the winner by unveiling their favorite dinner. Awarding additional prizes and/or privileges is up to your family.

There are plenty of creative ways to do your measuring. See what you think about these ideas and then brainstorm what else you could do . . .

"Ad Dash" (mentioned earlier in "Challenge") is an example of "out-of-the-box" timing, where you're racing against the time it takes for TV commercials to run.

Throw a treat into the oven, guaranteed to fill the house with drool-inducing smells (brownies!). The minute the treat goes in the oven, everyone races to complete their task(s). You can return to claim your share of the treat as soon as you're done.

You can measure your child's behavior at any time, simply by announcing you're going to perform an attitude scan. Clap your hands together, then open them - palms out - like a movie producer does when they're, "framing" their next star.

Move them (your hands - not your child!) up and down - as if taking a reading. Then, clap again. The scan is over. It's time for the readout.

Slow separate your palms and keep going - moving your hands outward (the way fishermen shows his fish was "this big"). You might pretend to get stuck a few times and then go on. Of course, sound effects add to the fun. Hands that don't spread very far = you've got some work to do. Hands that go way out = Nice job!

Optional: You could end any scan by taking those extended arms and giving an encouraging hug!

"Chore Monster" is a brand-new website that's all about measurability and rewards. It's easy to use, colorful and has some humorous monsters thrown in for fun. It's easy to set up and schedule each task along with its point value. You can even easily add pictures.

You also set up clear rewards and their point values that kids can work towards.

Those rewards can be anything from big wish, list items that can be bought, to more attainable goodies, to things that don't cost anything:

- ✓ an extra ½ hour on the computer/TV
- ✓ a favorite meal
- ✓ a later bedtime
- ✓ an outing to a favorite spot
- ✓ or – our daughter's personal favorite – "Slave-Mom" (or Dad) where we take over one of her responsibilities

When it comes to buying rewards, I like to equate one point to one penny – so when Jannine wanted to buy a Kindle book that cost $2.99 – she had to earn 300 points.

I've got two bonuses I like throw in there:

50 points if all tasks for the day are completed.

50 points if all chores are done without any reminders.

Chore Monster is extremely flexible, so you can set this up however you see fit. It's a tool that gives very clear, measurable parameters that help kids see the goal and how to get there.

Recently, mobile apps have been introduced to make it even more easy for parents to submit and approve chores and kids to find out what points are available for the day and report in when they're done.

There is an opportunity to upgrade at a very fair price where kids can earn more monsters and get to go to a carnival. It's not necessary, but Chore Monster has been very generous to offer this outstanding service for free so doing the upgrade if you can is a great way to say, Thanks!"

If this sounds like your kind of Monster, than head on over to www.ChoreMonster.com.

Advancement

Let's say I were to pay you $1,000 a day to go out to the beach and dig a hole along the shoreline - right where the waves came in. You might be fast and get down a foot or two before the water rolled in and filled your hole right back up.

You'd expend your energy - giving up a little more of your life - day after day, to dig that hole that won't stay a hole. How long would you last?

Unless you had some really powerful outside motivation (perhaps you're digging to earn money to build an orphanage or pay medical bills to save your parent's life) - wouldn't it be tough to stay in this pointless game?

Don't we need to feel like we're moving forward? - That we've got purpose and direction in our lives?

Even - and perhaps especially - addicted video gamers feel this. They may sit for hour after hour late into the night, staring at a glowing screen - lost in a virtual world. They may not have a job. They may skip personal hygiene. They may appear totally rudderless in the "real" world.

But they are, in fact amazingly focused. From their point of view, they are action figures with a job to be done no matter the obstacles. They will do whatever it takes (both in the virtual and real world) to pull off their quest. It's all about getting to the next level.

The designers of these games know that each challenge must be compelling and - (this is key) - short and believably do-able. Once a task is completed, a new arena of play is introduced - one that ratchets up the level of difficulty just a bit each time.

Then, it's like watching goofy YouTube videos - it's hard to stop at just one.

So, hours and even days later kids (and that includes kids in grown-up people skins) are rewarded for their substantial investment in time. They develop powerful sitting muscles - and get the bragging rights to having reached level 203 along with a sack of points, tokens and titles. All of this feeds that "need to succeed."

Of course, all of this glory vanishes when a thunderstorm knocks out the power grid.

Imagine the real, heroic potential if all that raw desire to advance and achieve along with all the time and money now spent on games were diverted to challenges like solving the world hunger problem, figuring out how to have unlimited clean energy . . . and conquering clutter around the house!

There are at least 2 ways to provide opportunities to advance right in the home.

The first way is to set up the kind of advancement markers - honors if you will - found in video games like levels, points, tokens and titles.

What if you were to rank chores by level of difficulty and made it an honor to be achieved. This can be tailored, of course. Here's one example:

Clearance Level

Code Green

Authorized to . . .

Put away toys

Pick up trash

Clear the dishes

Sweep the floor

Clean up bedrooms

Clearance Level

Code Magenta

Authorized for . . .

Washing machine operations: Must demonstrate the ability to sort dirty clothes correctly, pass the hidden crayons in the pocket test, and be able to handle the machine itself correctly.

Dishwasher tech: Must be able to load to maximum capacity and demonstrate an understanding of the control panel.

Dryer Detail: Demonstrates an ability to load and run this equipment. Must be able to match socks correctly, know folding techniques (you even could throw in origami towel folding), and know the owner of each item of clothing. Magenta Clearance personnel may have access to TV while performing this task.

Vacuuming: Will be rated on ability to tackle difficult areas - under furniture, behind doors, along walls, as well as maneuvering skills and waste disposal.

Mending: Able to thread a needle and repair a broken button and torn clothing.

CLEARANCE LEVEL

CODE GOLD

Authorized for . . .

Car Detail: Must pass training for washing and vacuuming.

Lawn Mower Ops: Show understanding of safety training and be able to navigate curbs and edges. There is a strength requirement to dispose of clippings properly. Gold Clearance has access to mower to earn money in the neighborhood.

Window Washing: Must demonstrate ability to use sprayer and squeegee as well as safety procedures with a ladder. Windows must pass clarity inspection. (This task could be placed in Level Two if using Microfiber, silver cloths)

Motorized Hedge Trimmers and Edgers: Proper safety precautions and ability to use these restricted tools properly

Each level should be tied to additional benefits. Think - a larger allowance, extra privileges, even a prop such as a pin, ring, hat or some other token of advancement. You might even want to make up some fun ceremony or special meal when a new level is reached and a token awarded.

You may also award advancement points according to how well a task has been performed. Titles may be awarded in connection with these points. You could go from the humorous to the glorious. Check these out:

100 points - RAG ROOKIE

500 points - DUST DEMOLITION

1000 points - ROOM RANGER

1500 POINTS - BLACK NINJA

2000 points - ORDER OF THE WHITE GLOVE

It'd be fun to hear what titles your family dreams up and what ideas you come up with to provide that sense of advancement. Please drop on by and share at the www.cleaning-games.com/forum page and check out the "Earning A Rank For Cleaning Skills" section.

You can pick up printable tools to go with these activities at the site's Toolbox page.

The second way to satisfy the desire to achieve and advance is to let your kids actually affect real change in the home. It's such an important ingredient, that it's got its own jar - a great segway back to the Pantry where we'll check out "empowerment and strategy"

Empowerment and Strategy

These were once separate jars, but they're just so "salt and pepper" connected that I've put them together. empowerment is about gaining control. strategy is about what you do with that control. See what I mean?

Now, I have a confession. I loathe the game "Old Maid." You pick cards randomly from each other, hoping for a match so you can bank it and get rid of the cards in your hands before you end up with the dud "Old Maid" card. The person stuck in the end with that card loses.

Wow. I'm sorry, but there's just no thinking in this game. Everything is just so random - unless you count pushing one card higher than the others trying to get someone to pick it. Come on. A couple of blind, arthritic monkeys could play it and get the same results.

I honestly don't know how Old Maid has survived the decades - nor why my husband and daughter vote to play it when we have Friday Game Night (unless it's to see the look on my face that says "I'd rather eat Kibble.")

Empowerment, on the other hand puts you in the driver's seat and strategy lets you choose where you're going to go. Competitive sports and many popular games are bursting with opportunities for both:

- Will you take chances or play it safe?
- Will you misdirect your opponent or play straight up?
- What about timing?
- Who will you pass to?
- What formation will you run?
- Do you save your strength for an unexpected burst at the end or intimidate the other team with a full show of strength from the start?

When you win - you can take it to the bank - you've earned it.

Loose and you can go back to the chalkboard and rework your strategy for another shot at winning. There's always something new to try - always hope.

The arts of empowerment and strategy come into play with chores too.

Empowerment

At the end of "Advancement" I promised to talk about a second way to help a child satisfy their need to advance. Empowerment will do that every time. Kids love computer games because they're in charge. Win or lose - it all comes down to their own decisions.

Now, if you want to help satisfy the desire to achieve and advance - try letting them actually effect change in the home.

It can be a very simple gesture. For example, when I was a teeny, weenie tot, I remember my father taking me with him to pick out our first station wagon - and he let me pick the color: red or white. I went with the red.

To this day (many eons later) I still remember how important I felt because that all-important choice was mine and I was reminded every time we went anywhere, of how my parents respected my decision.

An easy way to help your child feel like they've got a say in their chores is to give choices. For example, "You can clean out everything lurking under your bed or rake the leaves . . . make lunch for everyone or mow the lawn . . . clean out the fish tank or build an underground survival bunker in the backyard . . .

Here's another way to empower a child so they understand that their choices are important and matter to you. Try brainstorming with your kids about what their ideal bedroom would be. Then, turn over control (perhaps with some guidelines) and help them work toward a room that's truly an expression of your child. You can let them earn each upgrade to their room as they show responsibility taking care of it.

Here's a few upgrade examples. Many of them can be made in very educational, satisfying projects. Just hit YouTube or Google and type "How To Make . . . (whatever it is you'd like to add to your home).

I've thrown in some "how to" links (please ignore the ads and any obnoxious music if you run into any) but there's plenty more where these came from.

If you are reading the hardcopy or audio book version of this book and want the "How To" and "Where To Buy" links, you can get them at: www.cleaning-games.com/shannon-suggests/

Now, here's those upgrade suggestions.

- Posters and pictures
- Rearrange the furniture
- Plants (Decorate the pots and start with seeds or go for something more exotic like a cactus or Venus Flytrap).

- Fish (For something even more cool there's Sea Monkeys and Triops - also known as the "Living Fossil"). You can also check out the animatronic "Magic Jellyfish."

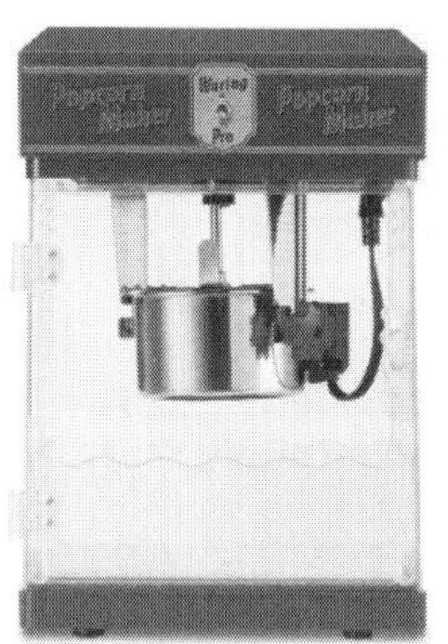

- A lava lamp
- A nostalgic popcorn machine
- A doorbell
- A rainbow or mural painted or posted on the wall
- Colorful pillows
- An intercom to the kitchen
- A fountain
- Glowing "Star Mural" on the upper walls and ceiling
- A Magic Crystal garden you can make or buy)
- An Ant Farm you can buy or one you make
- An animatronic Butterfly - or even Firefly - in a jar

Notice, I didn't say "A computer or TV." It's far safer to keep these electronics in the more public places of the house.

What upgrades would you recommend?

Please share with us on our site's forum page under "Room and House Upgrade Suggestions."

www.cleaning-games.com/forum/

You can go beyond the bedroom. Your family can brainstorm "next level" upgrades for the whole house and tie them to kids showing they can take care of what they currently have.

In fact, if you want to design your dream home and anyone wants to play "Interior Decorator" Trimble has a free, program with very easy video tutorials that will let you lay out your home in 3-D on the computer and let you add furniture and frills. It's called Sketchup and you can grab it here:

http://www.sketchup.com/intl/en/product/gsu.html

(There's a pro version, but this link is for the free one).

Kids can be awarded their own garden plot (or "pot" if you're short on space) where they pick whatever they'd like to grow, and the life of everything in that garden is completely in the hands of your child (come on, now - stop that shuddering! :o)

In fact, we've just been learning about "Fairy Gardens" where you make a very tiny habitat for little fantasy folk. It's a great exercise in creativity and can be done outdoors or in. Here's a few examples I put on Pinterest:

http://pinterest.com/adventureaisle/fairy-gardens/

A few home-wide upgrade ideas would be:

- A fun new appliance, like an ice-cream maker, for the kitchen
- A shower head and/or faucet with LED lights
- A game table
- A backyard "Zip Line"
- A ceiling fan
- Sky Lights
- Flowers
- Dwarf Fruit Trees
- A Piano Keyboard
- A Clubhouse
- A giant white-board . . . and you can really go big with white-board paint

- An Air Pogo
- A pet . . . Ooops! Did I let that slip out?!!!

These are just suggestions that range from free to saving up for some time. What goes on your family list will depend on your tastes and budget. The point - your kids will likely be much more motivated to care for a home that that gets better and even more fun because they're pitching in. It'll send a "loud-and-clear, over-and-out" message that their input really counts!

STRATEGY

For many years, Jannine's chore strategy was to stuff . . . stuff under the bed when it was time to clean her bedroom - and when we weren't looking. But, she's upped her game.

Now, she hangs her clothes according to color, she tosses in decorative frills, splashes on some fun fragrance and mixes it up with a dash of stealth so she can catch her parents off guard and watch them "pass out" in slow motion when we "discover" what she's been up to.

Here's a few techniques that have worked for us:

- **Clean an entire room in 5 minutes:** Simply round up everything that's out of place and put it all into just one spot (putting everything on the bed adds motivation since you can't sleep there until it's cleaned).

  It's a great morale booster to see a room look amazing so quickly! If you want a portable mess - throw everything into a sorting basket or onto a blanket. Now, you can take it completely out of the room to deal with while doing something else you like - say watching TV.

- **Round up . . . then divide and conquer**: Now, once you've rounded up everything into one place, it's much easier to sort through.

  For example: if you've got dirty dishes in a bedroom - it's far easier to go through one pile in one place, put those dishes all together and take everything down to the kitchen just once - v.s. multiple trips each time you come across yet another cup or plate. Same goes for dirty clothes, books, toys, papers, magazines, gum-wad collections . . . whatever lurks.

- **Ticket to Ride:** Just like trains and busses have a designated route, why not designate a box or sack for each part of the house? When you sort, just deposit each item in the container that's going where it needs to go. It's "divide and conquer." So - one box for the basement. . . one for the main floor . . . one for donations . . . one for the trash . . you get the idea. One box. One trip. Done.

- **Strategic placement:** Try fastening a small scrubbing cloth and a rubber glove to each bottle of cleaner with a rubber band. Put each bottle in handy places around the house and you won't have to go hunting for a rag or a glove when your toilet needs scrubbing. Everything will be right there so you can just get in and get out.

- **A Touch of Class:** One simple trick hotels, cruise ships and resorts use to ramp up the classy factor at no additional cost is "Origami Towel Folding." Now, you can bring this fun idea home, to create everything from cool fan designs to fluffy critters. Here's a link to a list of books on Amazon that cover not only towels, but also napkin and toilet paper art.

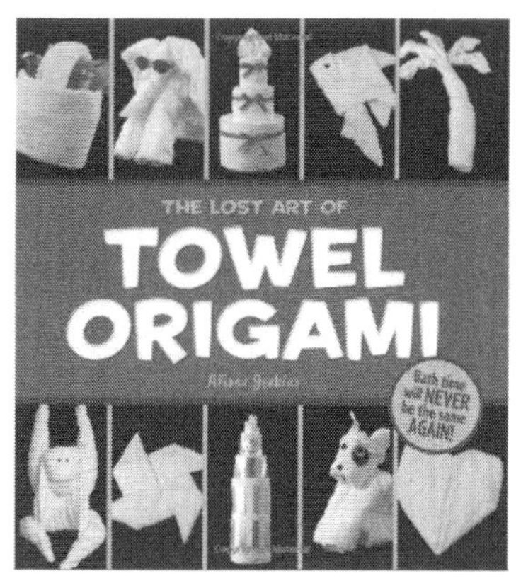

- **Junk Jail:** I just learned about this clever **strategy** - it's not my idea, it's just pretty nifty! You set up a basket or box as the "Clutter Jail" and when something isn't cleaned up - it goes in the Jail. To get something out of Jail, you must draw a game card with a task you must complete. Sometimes there's a "Get Out Of Jail Free" card.

You can drop by iMom to get free printables for this one.

http://imom.com/tools/training-tools/clutter-jail-tool/

(Thanks, to Brittany M. for putting me up to this!)

Now - these ideas are just scratching the surface when it comes to home cleaning strategy.

There's some terrific tactical masters out there who can help you and your family hone your approach, save you time and make your home look better than its looked in years. You've heard of the classic by General Sun Tzu "The Art of War" . . . well, my favorite General in the "Art of Chore" is Don Aslett.

I was a teen when I first saw him put on a workshop at our church. As I remember, he billed himself as "The World-Famous Cleaning Guy." He told very funny, inspirational stories to make the point that no matter what your profession in life - take pride in what you do.

He pointed out that anybody could look important - not hard - all you need do is roll up a long piece of paper and walk around with it under your arm the way an architect does.

To demonstrate what how he took pride in being a cleaning guy, he showed us his suitcase that he'd had designed to look like a toilet. He said it was very handy in airports when there weren't enough seats. "I'd much rather clean a toilet than a mouth," he said. "Toilets, most times, look a lot nicer inside . . . and they don't bite."

He had us so excited about the joys of housework that folks were lining up afterward to buy stuff like earrings that looked like tiny toilets . . . as well as his now, classic book "Clutter's Last Stand."

Since I first saw him, Don Aslett has taken his little cleaning company and turned it into a multi-million dollar trusted brand. He practiced what he preached.

One Amazon.com review reports, "His private label brand of cleaners, Don Aslett's Time Savers, are perennial favorites on QVC. Don has appeared on Oprah, as well as all the national shows and in the pages of every woman's magazine, from Real Simple to Cosmopolitan."

You can check out Don's stuff on Amazon for some terrific tips from the master cleaning strategist himself.

The Extraordinary

Riding a zip line. Reading a book that takes you to long-long ago and far-far away. Eating at Benihanas where they "perform" at a flaming table, doing acrobatic knife tricks with your meal. "Zorbing" (where they push you down a hill in a giant hamster ball). Disney World.

In one way or another almost all of us love to step out of the ordinary and escape into the extra (meaning "out of the") - ordinary.

A RUT
IS A GRAVE
WITH NO ENDS

What about work? Why not throw in extraordinary twists here too?

- Try turning off all the lights in the house and working with flashlights or a camping lantern.
- Clean house "handcuffed" to a partner. You can use an old nylon sock, a scarf . . . a tie that binds, but doesn't hurt.
- I knew one young man whose family would get up in the middle of the night to clean the house and then go out to breakfast together. They called it the "Whistle While You Work Party." (This one's not for the faint of heart!)
- Switch rooms! I read in one forum of a mother whose daughter liked to clean her brother's room, but not her own. Well - why not?! Not only is it easier on parents to let their kids clean their room of choice, but it's serious motivation to keep things put away for - say a big brother - who does NOT like to have his room cleaned by his little sister . . . We're talking leverage here!

- Pick an "out of the box" place to do a task - say - sorting socks under the table . . . or . . . what about filling your bathtub (and empty one is best!) with clean laundry and climbing in with it. Then "fold your way to freedom" - hopping out once all the folding and sorting is done.

- Have a D.A.R.E. (Disabled Achievement Recognition Experience) where you take on a disability while doing chores. Here's a few suggestions to get you rolling. Why not try . . .

  - ❖ . . . doing tactile tasks like preparing a meal or doing the dishes - blindfolded

  - ❖ . . . moving about the house by scooting along in a sitting position on the floor (to appreciate missing your legs)

  - ❖ . . . trying to get things done while sitting in a wheelchair (any office chair with casters will do).

- ❖ . . . limiting the use of even one arm, by tying it to your side
- ❖ . . . plugging up your ears - so rather than speaking - everything must be communicated in gestures. (Get ready for some comical charades-like communication!).

You can pick which disability you want to experience or draw one randomly. What other ways can you simulate what a disabled person faces daily?

I've got a forum for this one too!

It's at www.cleaning-games.com/forum under the "Take A DARE" section.

Excitement!

What really "makes your socks roll up and down?!"

Is it curling up with the next installment of "The 39 Clues" series? . . . How about watching the SuperBowl? . . . Catching a 17-foot Marlin? . . .Taking on the "Tough Mudder?" . . . donning a Wingsuit and jumping from a cliff? . . .

Winning the State Science Fair Competition> . . . That week before your 16th birthday? . . . Inventing the world's first fur-lined bathtub? . . . Listening to Mozart's "Queen of the Night Aria?" . . . Propping yourself at the bow of a ship and shouting, "I'm the King of the World!"?

As a student, I learned of one man who got a thrill from sneaking into someone's house and going through every room without getting caught. He never stole anything (at least at first) - he just had an extreme craving to crank up his adrenalin.

With the help of a Recreational Therapist, they found a better outlet and he became a maniac, champion skier.

To each his own . . .

And because of that, I'll be honest - at this point, I've written everything else for this book, but have been skipping over this section again and again. I've been log-jammed on this ingredient. That wide variety of examples above are just tip of the iceberg.

Excitement is just so personal. Everyone finds it in so many unique ways.

I've realized that what I can do is boil down this ingredient into at least five parts - perhaps even phases. See what you think:

1. Mystery - The thrill of the unknown

2. Anticipation - The thrill of knowing something is coming

3. Adventure - The thrill of discovery

4. The Hunt - The Thrill of pursuing your discovery

   . . . or avoiding being discovered.

5. The Jolt - The thrill of having your insides turned . . . out (for a physical Jolt - say a roller coaster) or getting emotionally "revved up."

Now we can take these parts of excitement and put them to work.

So - let's get to it! Time to bring excitement to chores!

Let's just brainstorm in no particular order:

Adding music is one of the easiest ways to provide excitement.

We'd be in danger of swallowing our head yawning watching a lot of these reality shows without that suspenseful, tense music!

Think of the movie Jaws without that "Dun-Nuh. Dun-Nuh. Dun-Nuh . . . Nuh . . . Nuh . . . NU . . .NUH . . . NUH . . . NUH . . ." music that lets you know that shark is about to have lunch.

Or what if they played Barney's "I Love You" theme song during a wrestling match? It'd be like trying to envision Martha Washington scuba diving. Music can have such a dramatic impact on the way we take in the world around us, can't it?!

And throwing on favorite high-energy music can bring a Jolt to a job. Question is - whose favorite music?!

To get you started, here's a link to Radio WUHU (Read "Wooooo Hooooo!") on the Cleaning-Games.com site where I've set up an "Adrenalin" channel with a variety of "Pump-It-Up" music.

From there, you can use Grooveshark.com to set up your own channel with your own favorite tunes for free . . . if you'd like.

Ever play "No Bears Are Out Tonight?" - It's a nail-biter of a game where one person is chosen to be the bear who hides somewhere outside. The rest of the group goes around together looking for the bear.

When they get close enough - the "Bear" jumps out and tries to tag anyone and everyone before they can reach "base." Those who get caught, become bears. So the "woods" get fuller and the group gets smaller with each round. Played in the dark - it's a heart-pounding thing!

Now, this thrill of The Hunt and Mystery can be used while cleaning.

What if one person were to hide somewhere in the house while everyone else closed their eyes and counted to 50. Then, the group would spread out doing quick, easy chores (dusting, wiping out a sink, sweeping, taking out the trash . . .), not knowing when the "bear" was going to pop out. They could be hiding under a bed, behind a curtain, on the other side of a door . . .

For safety's sake, perhaps rather than trying to jump out and tag someone inside a house - a spray bottle or squirt gun could be used. If the bear "sprays" you - you become a bear too. Everyone left would return to base . . . and all the bears (each with a spray bottle) would hide again.

The person who wins would not the one who got caught last. - but the one who did the most chores before getting caught.

You can bring on both Mystery and Adventure by hiding a "treat treasure" somewhere in the house. Then hide a clue to the treat's location in each place where kids will be cleaning. They'll find the clue while working, and once they've completed that task, they can move on to the next area where they can find the next clue.

Alone, the clues shouldn't amount to much, but combined - they'll reveal the "treat treasure."

Clues can be as simple as writing out or even drawing a map to where the treats are on a piece of paper and then tearing up the map so that each section is part of the clue. Clues could also be numbered, step-by-step directions.

What about a cleaning version of "Musical Chairs?" Start out with enough cleaning tools for each player (more is better here so you might want to invite friends). Play music while everyone cleans with their tool (broom, sponge, squeegee, dust rag, etc.). While they're cleaning, quietly take away one person's tool and then stop the music.

That's the signal to switch jobs! Everyone must immediately put down their tool and run to find another one so they can stay in the game doing a new job. It's "The Hunt" again!

Players can move about the house as long as they're using their tool to clean something. That makes it harder for the other players to find that tool the next time the music stops.

Each round another tool is removed until there's only one person left with the final tool.

Kids who do not have a tool become referees. They watch the other players to try to catch them not working. If they do - the kids switch places and the kid without the tool is back in the game. Referees also decide which tool gets taken next and can help turn the music off.

Check out the "Workin' Tunes" channel on Radio WUHU I put together, if you'd like to have your music already set up for this game. www.cleaning-games.com/home/radio-wuhu/

Consider kidnapping your child from time to time in the middle of a cleaning assignment, and taking them out for a fun outing of your choosing. It's a random reward they'll grow to anticipate. The more they help, the greater the chance of being "kidnapped." A blindfold is optional!

Socialization

Twenty years ago, Faith Popcorn (isn't that a fun name?!) wrote her bestseller "The Popcorn Report" - a book that predicted where society was going by looking at the current trends.

One of her most famous glimpses into the future was something she called "Cocooning." She and her team defined it as " . . . the impulse to go inside when it just gets too tough and scary outside . . . Cocooning is about insulation and avoidance, peace and protection, coziness and control - a sort of hyper-nesting."

She pointed out the sharp increase in sales of VCRs and video tape rentals (remember those?!), microwave popcorn, pets (including "rent-a-cat" services) and even 'Video Fireplaces."

Everything in 1992 seemed to be pointing to a collective "hunkering down" in the United States. She talked about the "Armored Cocoon" (more defensive weapons at home) and 'Wandering Cocoons" (about having it all in your vehicle).

At the end of the chapter, she hit on "The Socialized Cocoon" - about inviting guests into our nests. She called it "Huddling and Cuddling" and - selectively inviting a few close friends in. She suggested we'd even overlook our differences to form special interest groups and such. She was saying, that even though we'd be closing down, we'd still be reaching out.

Twenty years ago, how could even the talented, trend-surfer Faith Popcorn have predicted the explosion in the social cocoon when we

Who could have known that FaceBook would grow so quickly that if it were a country, it would be the third largest in the world (after China and India)? . . . Or that YouTube (as of this 2012 writing) receives more than 72 hours of new video content uploaded every minute? . . . Or that Pinterest - the neat-stuff, image-sharing service would break the record for fastest growing site by jumping to over 11 million users in about a year and half's time.

Twitter . . . LinkedIn . . . Badoo, . . . Orkut. . . . Flickr. . . . CafeMom. . . . More and more ways to say, "Howdy There!" are emerging every day.

The poet John Donne hit the proverbial nail right on the head when he penned, "No man is an island entire of itself; every man is a piece of the continent, a part of the main."

No doubt! - No matter how harsh and scary the world gets, we always have, and we always will, find a way to reach out to each other. It seems our appetite to be sociable is just plain, old insatiable.

So, how to cook socialization - into work? The same way the seasoning Chili Powder is made up many spices (dried chilies, garlic, oregano, cumin, coriander and cloves), there are multiple parts to socialization. When we break it down and understand each part, it's easier to come up with great recipes for turning work into play.

Here are a few reasons folks love to socialize.

There are probably more:

Team Identity - A sense of belonging. It's high 5's, uniforms, nicknames, working together as a group.

- Pick out or even design your own family uniform. Could be as simple as matching baseball caps and T-shirts, and wear them while getting things done around the house or even performing an act of service in the community.

- Come up with a family cheer. It could be something simple like: "Meyers rock the house!" Or hold up a finger for each member of your family (so if you've go 2 parents and 3 kids - hold up five fingers) and shout, "We're Number One!"

- Come up with nicknames tied to strengths when it comes to work. You may want to say only members of the family can use these names. For example:

  "**Riptide**" - someone who loves to clean with water / do laundry

  "**Sweet Feet**" for the teammate who can move very fast when cleaning.

  "**Grizzly**" one who's great at lifting large, heavy loads

  "**Ghost**" if you've got someone who's able to get things clean when no one's looking.

Spectators - It's 'Look Ma! . . . and look everybody else too.' Whether it's earning a place on "The X-Factor," having the bleachers full when your team is playing, or having an audience for your blog, - in one way or the other, the chance to be recognized is a big deal.

- It's easy to set up a cleaning competition, where only two race and the rest of the family cheers. In fact, you could even get down to just one kid against the clock.

- Capture any cleaning activity on film and encourage kids to ham it up for a laugh - or go for the "Extreme Clean" approach to impress with speed and agility.

If you know how to do simple video editing - it's easy to "go slow-mo" or do the opposite and show chores being done at high speeds. Add funny or cool music and your family will have a ball watching the replays.

It's likely your computer may already have free video editing software on it, like Microsoft's "Movie Maker" or Apple's iLife "iMovie." YouTube also has some simple editing tools.

If you don't have these or you want to want to ramp it up a bit, one place you can go to pick up a free 30-day trial of high-quality, easy-to-use video editing software is Corel's VideoStudio. It even has free tutorials you can watch.

- It's VERY easy to set up a website or blog these days! Why not show off your cleaning capers online? One of my favorite places to make your own website is www.Wix.com. Another good one is www.Weebly.com.

If my eight-year-old could make beautiful sites with streaming video in no time - so can you! It's easy. It's fun. It's free!

And by all means - please show and tell your site with us at our site! Having the chance to see your ideas in action can be very helpful to the rest of us!

Recognition - It feeds that sense of importance and it mainly comes from others (although there are a few who get it from their mirror). Some will rise to great heights while others will stoop to despicable acts just to be recognized. It's all the different degrees of fame.

- Consider holding an Evening of Thanks to everyone who's helped fix up the house (especially after a big project like painting or landscaping). Let your kids take turns sitting on a homemade "throne" in the middle of a room and give them a crown (aluminum foil works great!).

  Then, let everyone else take turns sharing what they think is the best thing about that person. Take turns sitting on the throne! It feels pretty good up there!

- Make a family newspaper about all the fun things you're doing to clean up. Include stories and incidents that "brag up" each child's efforts. You can then share copies with friends and family. Makes a great keepsake too!

Support and Encouragement - It's one thing to be "seen" and a better thing to be appreciated. Whether we're going through success, failure or somewhere in between - it's hollow without someone there to travel the road together.

- Try taking before and after pictures and keep them in a "trophy book" to show off. Words may ring hollow at times, but seeing physical proof (especially if you throw in some colorful stickers) will help kids start to see themselves as "creatures of cleanliness."

- Make up your own kind of "High 5" that's just for members of your family. It could be a "complex" combination of hand-slaps, knuckle-knocks and hip bumps.

  It could be a giggle-inducer like the "Avon Lady . . . thingie" (I'm not sure what to call this!). Pretend your kid has a doorbell on their shoulder, or head or tummy) and repeatedly press the spot with your thumb while singing out "Bing Bong!"

- We do the "turkey" at our place, where one person holds up an open hand (for the tail feathers) while the other person makes a fist with the thumb sticking out (for the body and head) and we slap them together to make this symbol of thanksgiving!

- "Team-Tackle a challenge." I used to say to Jannine, "It's your room. It's your mess. You made it. You clean it." Seemed perfectly reasonable, but I realized that while I was winning the battle, I was losing the war. Yes, the room would get cleaned - but often with a lot of tears of frustration from one overwhelmed daughter. She was learning to hate cleaning her room.

  I found that if I supported her - if we turned on an audio book or some music we both liked, and worked away at a mess together, the whole experience was a lot more pleasant. She was learning work wasn't so bad after all.

  And now, she won't let me help her clean her room anymore because she likes to fix it up her own way and surprise me. Do I take it personally that I've been (temporarily) kicked out of my daughter's room like this? . . . Are you kidding?!!

Rivalry - It's the child of the "challenge" and "social" ingredients.

Have you heard of "Triangulation?" As a social term, it means that rather than "you vs. me," it's "we vs. it (or them)." It's a way of drawing two opposing forces - like siblings - to unite them against a common opponent.

One tremendous example of Triangulation happened on 9/11. It was a terrible day in the face of great evil . . . but it was also the day that Democrats, Independents and Republicans forgot the lines drawn in the sand. And that spirit of unity spread worldwide as nation after nation dropped their differences and stood together against terrorists.

Rivalry works another way. Do you remember the wonderful movie "Soul Surfer?" It's the story of Bethany Hamilton a teen who loses her arm to a shark and fights to make a comeback in surfing competition. Bethany had plenty of folks who felt sympathy for her, but she also had a bitter rival who wouldn't let up even after the attack.

At Bethany's lowest point she thanked this rival for forcing her to work harder - to be her best while others wanted to go easy on her. This rival had inadvertently helped Bethany and they ultimately became good friends - not despite - but because of that rivalry.

- Use any of the activities addressed in the competition section of challenge for this one.

Validation - It's just the satisfaction of being heard and needed. It's why teens will talk to or text each other for hours. It's why a senior in a nursing home craves a visit even from a stranger. It's why debate is a popular sport. It's a great motivator for volunteer work.

To be honest, I struggled to come up with a specific activity for this one and have concluded that it's because it's a special force that can be found throughout any worthwhile activity.

This may sound trite, but I don't care.

The easiest way to dish out Validation is with a listening ear and a warm smile (and these can be pulled off in so many ways - across separators like deafness and distance).

Information - We also socialize to learn from each other.

Have you ever been involved in a service project where everyone is there doing a good thing . . . in near silence? It's so easy to become so engrossed with the task at hand that we forget to communicate!

So, while you're side by side, working away - or at home - here's some open-ended conversation starters where everyone gets to learn something. Why not take turns pretending to be a reporter?

- What book are you reading right now? Can you tell about it?
- If you had a million dollars - what would you do with it?
- Pretend this broom is a magic wand that can send you anywhere. Where would you like me to send you? Why?

- What do you remember from when you were little? Would you like to hear about some of the funny things you did?

- If this room began to shake right now and we found ourselves in the middle of an earthquake - what would you do? What about a fire? What about a visit from Dennis Rodman?!

- Can you describe a typical day at school?

Another fun way to while away the time while you're working, is to do brain-teasers together. It's a verbal game where a riddle is presented by one person and the other may ask "Yes" or "No" questions to draw out more information and deduce the answer. Often, brain-teasers trick you into assuming one thing when the answer is actually something entirely different.

Here's a sample. If you want to try to solve this brainteaser, you may want to cover the rest of the page now so you can reveal the clues and the final answer one line at a time. You might even want to get someone else to peek at the answer so you can pepper them with "Yes" or "No" questions.

Here we go!

BRAINTEASER

A man is running home,

sees a man with a mask

and runs back the other way

as fast as he can.

What happened?

CLUE #1

There are a lot of people watching this.

CLUE #2

The man with the mask has something in his hand.

CLUE #3

If you can figure out what the mask looks like, you'll know exactly what happened.

CLUE #4

If you figure out what the man with the mask was holding, all will become clear.

CLUE #5

You could have been the man in the mask.

CLUE #6

The man is NOT running to a house - he's running "home."

CLUE #7

This home has no bathrooms or kitchen.

CLUE #8

If the man with the mask weren't holding the thing in his hand the other man would have run all the way home.

ANSWER:

This is a baseball game.
The man in the mask is the catcher.
(Not a crook holding a gun).

"Home" is home-plate.
(No bedrooms or fireplaces anywhere!).

The man running home ran back the other way
because the catcher was holding the ball
and would have put him out.

For a huge collection of Brain Teasers, there are quite a few books out there or you can pick up MindTrap® - a game that has hundreds of brain-teasers written on cards.

We don't just learn from talking, of course. Doing things together is a great way to learn new skills.

This isn't going to sound original because it's something most parents do by instinct - but involving your kids in more grown-up chores is great social-sport.

It really is a tremendous experience to crawl under a car and change the oil together, or to cook a complex meal with the help of even very young children, or verbally talk a kid through pulling together a floral arrangement, or watch a "How to fix your washing machine" video on YouTube and then tackle the project as a team.

Memories - Positive social experiences remembered are among our greatest treasures in this life. The best memories are the ones shared with those you love.

- Break out your old "Trivial Pursuit" game board and write your own quiz questions on 3x5 cards about the chores you've done.

  Examples:

  Where do we keep the broom?

  What color are the sponges in the kitchen?

  Which person likes to eat the leftovers when they clear the table?

  Who can carry 8 bags of groceries on one arm?

  What is written on Mom's favorite cooking apron?

  Usually we break out the camera for the unusual -- to remember something out of the routine. With all the different options you've got in this book - and hopefully, the ones you dream up for yourselves, keep in mind that when you bring the fun to work you've got "FUN-derful" things happening right in your home. So make sure you catch them!

We benefit from looking back at the past.

I remember as a kid, we once had a lesson about how everyone wins when we pitch in. We loaded Mom up with clothes, a broom, towels and anything else we could find and scattered junk all about. Then, Mom whipped out her best exhausted pose. "Click."

Then we took another picture of all 5 kids helping pick up the mess to buy more playtime with Mom. "Click."

Now, we had ourselves a family classic pair of pictures.

It taught a lesson literally in a flash that has stayed with every one of us - even 30 years later. The image of Mom draped with everyone's junk, is now permanently etched in our brains. And we know there's a better way than leaving it all up to one parent.

NOT my Mom (she's cuter!)

Props

What does a tennis racquet, a tutu, and a checker have in common? You've already read the label on this jar, so - world's easiest quiz!

Props are the physical objects that bring much of the fun to a game. They may be essential, like - the ball. They may fuel the fire of imagination like backdrops and costumes. They foster a team spirit like uniforms and big, foam " We're #1" fingers to wave about.

Props can be used to bring the fun to chores too.

There are just so many props connected to cleaning, that I'm going to steer away from talking a lot about the obvious props - like brooms, mops, vacuums and such . . . except to say that they don't have to be boring. You can liven them up by letting your kids name them the same way they'd name a pet. Our lawnmower is "Big Red." The toilet brush - "Mister Swirley." The broom - "Tango." The vacuum . . . Rrrrrrumba!

And would you be open to letting your kids decorate your cleaning props (especially the ones that go out of sight after they're used)? Could your kids draw eyes and a big mouth on a dust pan? How about wrapping colorful duct tape around a mop handle? Garbage cans make great place to paint masterpieces.

If you've got the money - you might even want to consider giving each child their own tools to keep, name and decorate. They could be awarded at an advancement ceremony or you could just go to the store and let them pick out their own tools.

Onward. Let's talk about props that normally don't come up when it comes to cleaning . . .

Blacklights. Did you know - that a blacklight can detect hidden messes? This year (2012) the Best Western hotel chain is starting a new program where housekeepers now begin their cleaning with the lights off.

They use black lights to look for rodent contamination and organic substances like hair, blood, urine, assorted bodily fluids, and other "goodies" that are normally invisible to the naked eye. In some places (not Best Western) they're even used to spot scorpions.

Was that too much information?

Yes - it's gross to think about these lurking messes, but it's also like having superpowers to be able to see things others can't with the help of a blacklight.

I recommend blacklight flashlights. They're inexpensive and much more durable than the fluorescent tubes. There are even 3-way flashlights with a regular light, an ultraviolet / blacklight, and a laser light (although you don't want to give laser to kids who might wave them in a sibling or pet's eyes).

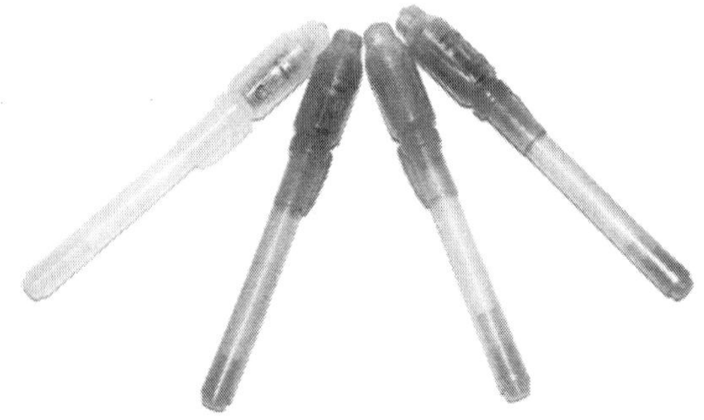

And just for your "Gee Wiz File," blacklights are also used by the police to investigate crime scenes, as well as the invisible ink on license plates and dollar bills.

Microfiber-Silver Cloths. I'll be up front - these aren't cheap. But they are amazing! They're an ultra-microfiber that's got silver woven into the material. They pay for themselves because you don't need to use cleaning chemicals with these - just water. I think less chemicals around the house make them healthier to boot.

Say you to accidentally smeared butter on your window or mirror (and who hasn't? :o) One of these clothes will not only slurp the butter up, but you can go on to wipe the rest of the glass, follow up with a polishing cloth and end with a window so clean it looks like it isn't there. And these things are FAST! You can clean an entire sliding glass door set in under 5 minutes.

They also don't get squishy and stinky after many uses because bacteria and silver don't like each other, so you only rarely need to wash these clothes. I found this witty consultant's demo on YouTube.

"Wearables." Nothing says, "I'm on the job" more than a uniform - or some other sort of official-wear. They can also foster a sense of "team" and honor for rank advancements. Try a small utility-belt for example, where kids can hang squeegees, sponges, small bottles, gloves and so on. Other items that can be personalized might include:

- An apron with lots of pockets
- A baseball cap
- Rubber gloves
- An armband
- A ring
- A badge

Humor & Playfulness

Don't you love to watch commercials on TV?!

Me neither.

. . . except . . .

When they're funny.

Tough ranchers herding kitties . . . A vacuum that works so well, it sucks the neighbor living down below up to their ceiling . . . or break-dancing babies selling Evian water - those kind of ads, get our attention and invite us to watch them over and over because they don't feel like they're trying to make us look at their product - they're just fun.

Humor and playfulness can make anything fun . . . well . . . almost anything. If I were having heart surgery, I wouldn't want my doctor launching into a comedy monologue or a tickle-fight.

But spicing up work with a dash of humor - It's a no-brainer.

The reason work and humor don't show up together that often is because:

1. Most of the time people aren't in the right frame of mind. What's funny about work when you're in the middle of it?

2. Most of us don't consider ourselves comedians and wouldn't know what to say or do to be funny even if we wanted to.

Yet, it's actually very easy to bring laughter to work around the house. One of the simplest ways is to listen to the humor of others while you're working.

I've set up "Radio WUHU" (read "Wooo Hooo!) on our website full of fun and funny songs (all G-rated) that will have others wondering what your laughing about as you clean the toilet. You can find it easily at:

www.cleaning-games.com

Here's a sampling of some of the songs I've got for you:

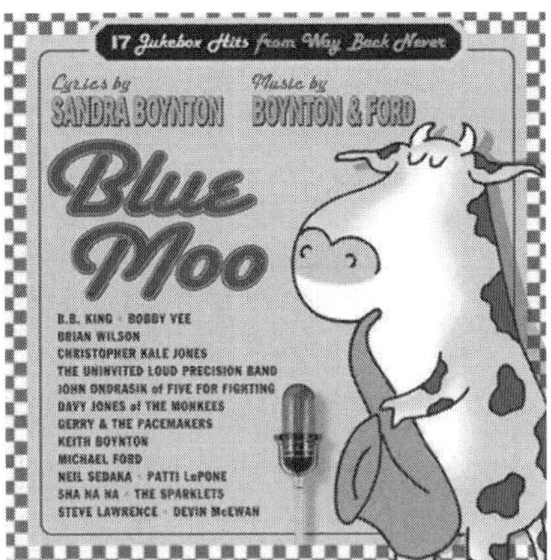

Sandra Boynton's stuff - Yes, the famous greeting card creator is also a terrific songwriter (one of my favorites!) who's had a host of stars perform her music.

(If you're reading this book on a mobile device that can get you to the internet, you should be able to listen to this sampling. Just click to listen!)

- Tickle Time
- BusyBusyBusy (sung by Kevin Kline)
- Nobody Understands Me (sung by Meryl Streep)
- I Like To Fuss (sung by Patty LuPone)
- I Need A Nap (sung by "Weird Al" and Kate Winslet)

Beethoven's Wig - a collection that introduces kids to classical music by adding funny lyrics (and yes - the album also lets kids enjoy the originals in their pure form)

- Just for Elise - Fur Elise
- Beethoven's Wig - 5th symphony by Beethoven
- Surprise Symphony - Haydn's Symphony No. 94 Surprise
- Drip, Drip, Drip - Pizzicato from Sylvia, Delibes
- Franz Listzt the Famous Pianist

Of course, there's tons of fun Oldies

- Purple People Eater
- Beep Beep
- Guitarzan
- Gimme Dat Ding

- I Love Onions
- Mah Na Ma Na

And here's just a few random goodies

- Peanut Butter and Jelly Song
- Billy Joe McGuffrey
- Stalking Song
- Jackie Chan

If you can think of songs that I've missed that need to be included on Radio WUHU, "please do tell!" Just go to the Forums page on our site (www.cleaning-games.com/forum), and share your favorites in the "Song Suggestions" section.

Also! If you'd like to set up your own Radio Station with your personal funny favorites, www.Grooveshark.com will let you have complete control over what's on your playlist and it's free.

I do have to point out one caveat. From time to time, they'll post an ad that is NOT family friendly. It hasn't been very often (and less is more!) but there's an easy fix - just go into the preferences and check the option to remove adult- themes.

You can even use a particularly grating song as a penalty. "I Love Onions" comes to mind . . .

You can also go for recordings of clean comedians. YouTube has quite a few to get you going (some funnier than others). I looked for ones that that don't offend and that you don't need to see, so you can just listen while you work. I've set up a collection of them on the site. Here's a sampling. Again, if you've got a digital copy of this book, the links are live:

- Stan Freberg Presents The United States of America
- The Mom Song
- Abbott and Costello - Who's On First
- Brian Regan – I Walked On The Moon
- Danny Kaye - The Pellet With The Poison
- Tim Hawkins - The Home School Family
- Jim Gaffigan - Hot Pockets
- Bill Cosby - Dentists
- The Smothers Brothers - The Saga of John Henry
- Steven Wright – The Complete Works

It's easy to find more family friendly humor. Just go to YouTube and to a search for "Clean Humor."

One more thing - You don't need this, but it's been a great investment at our home. We splurged and bought wireless speakers for my husband's B-day. We set them about the house and dubbed the system "Radio Jensen."

Now, we can pipe something on the computer (or any other sound source) to anywhere in the house. We love being able to just turn on just one speaker or all of them, and listen to music, stories, news - the works! . . . while we work.

Another way to liven up the work and make an unforgettable memory is to tie a practical joke into the job.

I remember Bill Cosby playing one on kids during his show "Kids Say The Darndest Things." He slipped a speaker inside a bowl of fruit and then - from somewhere else - he spoke to the kids through that speaker - so it looked and sounded like the bowl of fruit was speaking to the kids. He had these kids talking rather "matter-of-factly" with the fruit. What could be more natural?

To pull this stunt off, you need a way to see (or at least hear) what's going on - and a way to project your voice from whatever you choose.

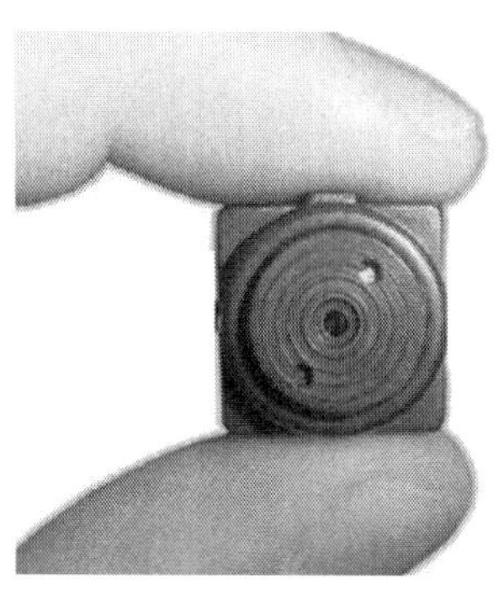

I did a variation of Bill's trick years later, when I hid a "Nanny Cam" (very cheap) and a wireless speaker into our elementary school's mascot: a knight . . . well . . . not a knight really – but it was a knight's suit of armor standing guard at the front door. Then, I hid in the front office across the way.

As kids of all ages went by, a suit of armor with my voice, reminded kids - to bring in cans of food for a charity drive the school was doing.

I also had them doing toe touches, and turning around in circles, and other silly stunts because - hey - who's going to argue with a talking tin can when it starts giving orders?!

You could pull off Bill's Bluff too. Does your cordless phone have an intercom feature (most do these days) or do you have a baby monitor? Another way to have both the camera and the voice, is to use the video chat in your smart phone (you'd need to have or borrow two of them).

Now, what if you were to hide "your voice" in the clothes hamper and make it complain about all the smelly clothes in it and - "Are you going to do something about it?!"

Or you could hide it in the fridge and when kids come to get a bite to eat, it could cry out to "drop that food!" and ask them if they've done their chores for the day. If they have - offer them a treat hidden in the back for just such special occasions - or - you can send them packing to get their chores done ("March! March! March!)

Do you have someone who takes forever to get their chores done? What if you were to tell them they can come down to dinner once they've finished their job. While they're working slowly away - string cobwebs all about the table and the people seated at it, then have everyone pretend to have fallen asleep while they were waiting. Imagine the reaction when your "victim" finally shows up at the table!

Pick a secret word that everyone but one person knows. Whenever that word is used while you're cleaning - use it as a cue to do something funny. So, let's say, if your word is "DISHES" each time anyone uses it, everyone that's in on the joke may swing their head around in circles a few times and then go back to work as if nothing had happened.

The person who doesn't know about the word will be utterly confused at the seemingly mass epilepsy attack (isn't that what it looks like when someone's trying to fight back laughter?!)

Another giggle-maker is to just do that copy-cat thing you do - just try it when you're working.

Let's say, you're folding laundry together and your daughter is copying you (or visa versa). See who can come up with the most outrageous way to sort and fold those clothes! Do you think she's going to laugh if she puts a pair of pajama bottoms on your head and you follow suit (By golly, I think that was a pun!). What if both of you went on to pretend the pants were hair and you were very vane - swishing your "hair" from side to side like a shampoo commercial. You could also dive under the pile, throw socks in the air, put something on backwards, do sock puppets . . . always one of you shadowing the other.

. . . Think about dancing with brooms . . . Dusting like a ballerina . . . washing the car like a kung-fu master . . . there are just so many things you can copy each other doing.

Yes - copy-cat-cleaning may take longer in the short run, but in the long haul, your kids will associate laughter and some great memories to those chores and think, "What's not to love about work?!"

Now, if you'd like to come up with your own "home-brew" cleaning humor, one way is to brainstorm with others - especially kids. Sometimes - all it takes to get the ball rolling is to say out loud, "Wouldn't it be funny if __???____ " and then as a group, throw out ways to finish the sentence." Pick your favorite and try it.

You can apply it to work by taking the half-sentence a bit farther and applying a work situation to your sentence: "Wouldn't it be funny, if you were taking out the trash (or any other chore) and all of a sudden

______**????**______! [*you fill in the blank*].

Here's a few examples of ways you could finish the sentence:

. . . the garbage bag rose up out of the can? (Best pulled off at night with the help of a fishing pole!)

. . . the voice of someone singing came from the trash bag? (easily done with a cordless phone in a Ziploc to keep it clean)

. . . a bunch of people were waiting to cheer enthusiastically, slap you on the back, shake your hand and sing your praises when you arrived at the garbage can.

You'd be surprised with what you can come up with when you let your brain play with this!

When you've got some fun, G-rated gags to share - please click on over to the Forums page (www.cleaning-games.com/forum) and let us in on your "evil genius!"

CHAPTER 4: "SECRET" FAMILY RECIPES

THE BOMB SQUAD

Three….

Two….

One…

GO!

"The launch pad rocketed us back in time ten minutes.

Our mission: To dismantle the bomb lurking somewhere in my sister's house before it exploded. I had been democratically elected as the mission's platoon leader.

It was my first mission, but my team were no rookies. They were confident in their ability to carry out the assignments I delegated to them and sprung into action as soon as it was time.

Our tactic to dismantle the bomb was simple- each of us took a room in the house and attempted to put everything back to where it belonged.

If we could set everything right, we'd neutralize the energy of the explosion in some sort of cosmic yin/yang reaction.

As platoon leader, I had been given the ability to add a power boost of five minutes to the expedition should we need it.

With music pumping in the background, we feverishly worked to bring order to chaos and avert the impending disaster.

My oldest sister, Shannon, rushed around the kitchen and bathroom with laser-like precision, pinpointing each article that was out of place and returning it to its rightful position.

Jannine, my niece, and I tag-teamed the rest of the rooms on the ground floor. When our ten minutes were almost up, we opted to use the power boost for five more minutes, finished the job and got back to the launch pad to return to safety.

Once there, we elected a new leader and repeated the process on the top floor of the house.

Living life with that kind of fun outlook can take some planning and some effort, but the outcome is so worth it. It was great to create some magic with my family and remind myself about the importance of **playfulness** in day-to-day life.

Next time it looks like a bomb has gone off in my house, I may just send myself in on solo mission."

- From Carrie Scott. Author of "Thirty and Flirty"

Thanks to my sister, Carrie – for sharing her eyewitness account of an actual Bomb Squad mission that she reported on from her blog (and that blog is a magical thing that I guarantee you'd have a BALL reading - no bias or anything . . .).

Bomb Squad is a family work/play recipe 30 years in the making.

This is the game that will have kids "begging for chores! "

Not only is it fun, but work gets done in half the time and many . . . many times, you'll find kids actually opting to work longer when they use the "Hyper-Boost" option. In fact, we've even had folks sneaking over to the timer to quietly add a few extra minutes to ensure a successful mission (Okay - it was me a few times . . . but I wasn't the only one!).

It's a game that began with our parents many eons ago. They'd have each of their of us six kids draw straws to see who would get to be the leader. Then they'd turn on our kitchen timer and we were off to do the bidding of the current kid in charge. It was fun then - and if you're into quick and easy - it's fun now too.

Bomb Squad is an evolution from those early days. It's still quick and easy to pull together, but now, it's been spiced up to use pretty much every jar in the Pantry of Fun . . . for an absolute BLAST!

How To Set Up Your Own Bomb Squad

Let's start with just the basic, raw ingredients of this game in "Adult-Speak."

1. Parents (or the kids) look around the house, for chores that can be done in 10 minutes, and write each on a card." How many points do you think that chore is worth? Write that on the card too.

2. The family gathers and picks a leader who hands out one card to each player.

3. The leader turns on a timer and some fun music.

4. Everyone cleans like a bunch of crazies for 10 minutes

   with a possible 5 minute extension.

5. Everyone reports back to base before the timer goes off.

Note: Players who finish early can go for extra points by asking for another card or helping someone else. A job completed earns points. Incomplete jobs may be finished in the next round or reassigned by the leader. Bonus points are awarded by vote to the family members who were the hardest working and most considerate.

Now, let's pull the **imagination** jar from the pantry and pour on a healthy, heaping, helping.

We're going to sprinkle in most of the other ingredients as well. Alright. Here's the game again.

It's exactly the same . . . only different!

(Don't worry about all the "Squad-Speak"!

There are translations at the end.)

Have you heard anyone say,

"It looks like a bomb went off in here!"?

Now - it's possible to actually reverse the effects of the blast

. . . if you're brave and quick!

Your Mission:

You have been summoned to join a crack team of professionals to travel back in time and stop that bomb!

Our Time Portal is a new, secret technology. The machine can safely run for 10 minutes. Your squad captain also has the authority to initiate a "Hyper Boost." It'll give you an extra 5-minutes. - Handy if a teammate is in danger of being left behind . . . or if the mission itself is in jeopardy!

You will each be given a mission card. Your card contains a key location in the house that's tied to the bomb. You must reverse the effects of the bomb to reverse the bomb itself. You have only 10 minutes to get in and get safely out. Keep your card for each mission completed to collect the points on it.

Squad Captain -If you've got younger or disabled teammates - make sure their mission cards and points are fair.

Your team will report to the Portal's launch pad. Chooses a squad captain by vote or random drawing. The captain then hands each team member their mission card. You may request a particular assignment, but the captain has the final say.

Players gather in a circle around the portal and link hands to form a star. The captain then activates the time portal.

Once the portal transports the team back in time, the entire squad moves out quickly to complete their missions. They must return and re-form the star-link before the portal shuts down. Only 10 minutes.

Hot Shots are players who complete their mission early and risk taking on another Mission Card for more points. They can check in with the captain for new orders or assist a teammate in need. They just have to get back before the Portal closes.

If one or more squad member isn't going to make it in 10 minutes - the captain can deploy the Hyper-Boost. It puts a strain on the time machine, so each captain gets only one Hyper-Boost - any more than that would be too risky!

Once the Portal returns you to your own time, the Captain does recon to see if the mission was a success. Squad members who complete their missions, bank their points.

Team members can (and should) share whatever points they think fair with Hotshots who helped them (otherwise they may be on their own next time!)

Squad-mates who don't complete a task are caught back in time - missing out on any points for that mission. Trying to join the star-circle doesn't work. - the Portal won't take them.

They must wait for the next mission to complete their task and collect their points - and even try to pick up some Hotshot points if they finish up early. Or . . . they can respectfully request a new mission from the new captain.

The Portal is capable of sending the team back for additional missions - so that each Bomb Squad member who wants a shot at being captain (no matter their age) will get it!

Once all missions have been run, the entire team votes (not for themselves) for the top captain (think - most fair and helpful) and top teammate.

"Grown-Up-Speak" Translations:

- Time Portal/Launch Pad: It's where every round of the game starts and ends. It can be any location in the house - a sofa, the stairs, a mini-trampoline, a blanket, your dog . . .

- HyperBoost: To add an extra 5 minutes to the timer.
    - Civilians mistakenly believe this term means feeding a teammate candy.

- Surveillance Sweep: To look around the house for places that need cleaning.

- Mission Card (Orders or Assignment): Chores and their point value written on cards. If you want to ramp up the "cool factor," invest in a cheap invisible ink pen that comes with a blacklight decoder to write these Mission Cards. Once made, these can be used again and again.

- "Players link hands" or "form a Star-Link": It's just everyone putting their hands together in the middle - the same way sports teams do it just before they go back into a game. (BREAK!)

- Activating The Portal: This is simply turning a timer and some music on to begin the 10-minute countdown.

If you'd like some sample Bomb Squad music you can use for your missions – you can crank up the "Adrenalin" program on Radio WUHU.

Of course, you can just play your own favorites. Music injects a LOT more energy into this game and you can just "crank" your player so it can be heard everywhere, or pick up those wireless speakers I mentioned earlier.

If, however, you live in an apartment with neighbors who have "bionic ears," it can be played out the opposite way - stealth mode - in total silence. In fact, you can even make the danger of being discovered by the neighbor play right into the game.

"Shhhhhhh!
"Be vewy, vewy quiet . . ."
- Elmer Fudd

- "Carry out orders :" Do those chores!
- "Before the Portal closes:" Before the timer goes off.
- "Once you team has returned to your own time . . .":
- After the round is over and the timer and music are off.
- "Captain does recon": The captain will check each player's work to see if the chore has been completed.
- "Portal is capable of sending the team back":

You can play more rounds – one for each player so everyone gets to be captain . . . or until there's nothing left to do!

How many Ingredients of Fun did you spot in this high-adrenaline approach to chores?

One optional "Prop" you might want to add is a "Bomb Squad" cap for each player. I've got a link for excellent wholesale prices at www.cleaning-games.com/shannon-suggests/

Benefits of Playing Bomb Squad:

- Everyone has a "Blast" making fun family memories!
- Kids gets to see messes from a parent's point of view when they act as captain of the squad and if they help with the "mission cards."
- Teamwork is a "big deal." Team spirit is rewarded.
- Kids get to practice leadership skills.
- The house gets very clean . . . very, VERY quickly!

Alright! On to another way to encourage kids to pick up after themselves . . . and have a positive attitude to boot:

The Happy Store

Do you know of parents who throw their kids things away if they don't pick them up? We all understand what they're trying to do - create a consequence that's strong enough to get their children's attention and hopefully save everyone a lot of nagging in the future.

It's a clear message:

"I MEAN business!"

But consider - doesn't this also teach kids that it's alright to throw away perfectly good things . . . to be wasteful?

Also - I know parents sometimes have to show "tough-love" but when we toss, a cherished bear or doll - we've thrown away a friend and risk the same kind of resentment that drove the little mermaid, to go see Ursula the sea witch.

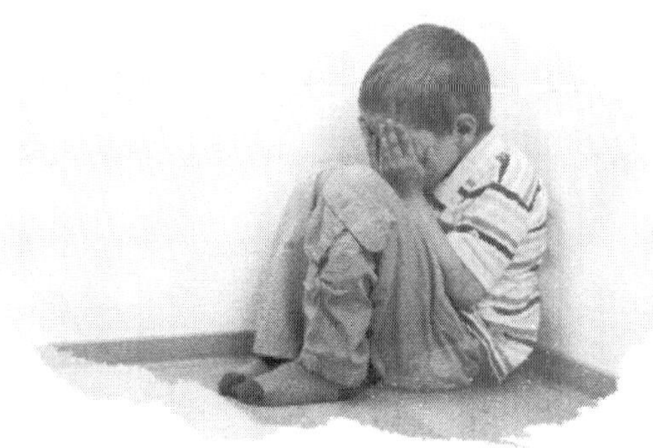

Why not - at very least - donate those items to a worthy cause, where those things will have a better chance of getting a good home than the seagulls in the landfill can give. At least, the message would be about charity and sharing.

But, there is another option!

"The Happy Store."

It's easy to set up and is a hit with kids!

(Although you absolutely have to change the name when you get into the "tweens" on up! How about "Redemption Island?" - as in the "island" counter in the middle of your kitchen - if you have one - to redeem your stuff).

Here's the way it works:

Head on over to the "Printable Play Money" website, and print up a big, old batch of bills (. . . just like the government does when it wants money!).

Explain to your kids that each day, they will be given an allowance of $10 in "Happy Bucks" and that you will be watching throughout the day for chances to award more.

Doing assigned chores will always earn Happy Bucks. The better the quality of the work, the higher the pay.

The goal here is to help kids appreciate what it's like to have a "real" job.

Making good choices is another way to earn Happy Bucks. It helps to define what good choices look like. Here's few examples:

- A "random act of kindness"
- A sunny attitude
- Singing around the house

- Offering to help
- Lending a hand to someone else with their job
- Practicing an instrument (although, if it's drums …mmmmm)
- Writing a grandparent a letter
- Submitting a positive review for a book (especially books on house-cleaning) that you like on Amazon.com! (Jeeeeest kidding . . . sorta :o)

Unlike the payment for chores, rewarding good choices should be kept random. Perhaps you can reward good choices with Happy Bucks most of the time in the beginning, but once you've got momentum, a good game plan would be to keep up the encouragement, but "ease off the throttle" on the Happy Bucks.

The goal here: Help your child discover the joy of doing something simply because it's the right thing to do.

Now - why just give them that 10 Happy Bucks each day?

Because, you may also need something to take away. If you run into bad behavior, you can subtract Happy Bucks from that daily allowance. So, even if your child doesn't feel like going out of their way to be good for a day - they've also got motivation not to "be bad."

It's your call, but this way has worked best for us.

The end of each day is the time each child is given their Happy Bucks for both chores and good choices.

Why should kids care about Happy Bucks?

Because once a week, they'll have a chance to spend them in the "Happy Store."

Here's how it works:

When a kid has left something lying around and had enough reminders - rather than throwing it away - that item now goes to the Happy Store, where it must be bought back . . . with Happy Bucks.

The more items that end up in the Happy Store, the more Happy Bucks a kid will have to earn to buy those things back

There's more.

Can you think of a time when you've gone shopping with your children, that they haven't asked for something (read: begged . . . whined . . . promised to pay you back . . . you know the drill). Me neither!

Rather than simply giving in . . . a compromise. You may want to let them choose one or two things that you'll buy. BUT . . . they don't get them right away. Rather - those new items also go into the "Happy Store."

We had generous friends, who would give Jannine a bag bulging with gifts every year until they moved. While we were thankful for their kindness, we were concerned about goodie-overload.

What would you do?

We didn't want to risk offending them by asking them to ease up on the toys, and by rights, those gifts were Jannine's.

We finally decided to give her a few of the gifts up front and put the rest in the Happy Store.

Each week, we'd pull out all the items - old and new, and lay them on our kitchen counter, along with a price tag for each. The pre-owned items, were set at 'thrift store prices" while the new items often just cost close to the same in Happy Bucks as they did in real dollars.

Jannine loved getting her gifts this far more than she did just having them simply handed to her. She felt very grown up getting to go shopping and spending her own "money" on real things. She valued them more - after all, she had earned them!

The Happy Store is a win for everyone. Parents get to teach instead of nag and don't have to play the "bad guy." Kids learn in a fun way to be more responsible and get to understand the value of a dollar to boot. They even get a chance to practice their math skills!

Peace and a positive relationship between parent and child is not only maintained, but improved by playing this learning game.

If you've got **props** like a toy cash register, a kid-sized shopping cart, shopping bags, or clerk aprons - this would be a great time to break them out!

Parents, and even siblings, posing as clerks add to the fun. Throw in phrases like, "Will that be all, Miss?" and "Thank you for shopping with us, Sir," and "We're having a sale today on used diapers," . . . and you're good to go!

You can tweak the recipe for this game any way you'd like.

Here's a few variations you might want to sprinkle on top:

- "Shoppers" must buy back all (or at least some) of their pre-owned possessions before they can buy anything new in the Happy Store.

- Any pre-owned items not purchased back by the original owner, after a set number of weeks, may become available for other family members to buy with their Happy Bucks.

- Used items that are not bought may eventually be rounded up and given to another person, family or charity. The family could even vote on where these items might do the most good.

- Parents themselves may choose to participate in the Happy Bucks program, where kids could try to catch them leaving things lying around or forgetting chores. Kids might even be given a say each night, as to how many Happy Bucks they think Mom and Dad earned.

THE AMAZING RACE - HOME-STYLE EDITION

Have you ever imagined yourself on the Hit TV show "The Amazing Race?" If you haven't - you must not have seen it! Surely, it can't be because you're put off by a little thing like having to shave your head or jump off a cliff dressed as a Teletubbie (you never know!)

If you haven't seen it yet, let me recap. Teams race from one country to the next trying not to be the last team to check and be eliminated at various stages of the game. The last team standing wins a million dollars.

Along the way, there are challenges each team must pass through. A few examples: Navigate a labyrinth full of rats, eat through 11,000 chocolates to find one with a white center, build a TeePee, Roll a cheese wheel down a hill in a flimsy wooden contraption, and search for a clue in a haystack (tons of haystacks, actually).

This Emmy Award-winning reality show is loaded with clues, puzzles, roadblocks, detours, penalties, and all-out-sprints to the finish line. It's an idea most everyone wants in on - even if there isn't a pot full of gold at the finish line. If you Google this, you'll quickly find pages and pages of ideas about how to host your own Amazing Race.

The twist here is to apply this incredibly successful recipe for fun - to housework. It's like swapping to wheat flour in a white bread recipe.

This concept is so flexible that there's an unlimited number of ways to go at it. It does take some preparation, but if your goal to help your kids learn to really enjoy work, than setting up and pulling off this activity is an investment your family will treasure for a long time to come.

Here's some guidelines to get the ball rolling:

Prep Work:

1. **Decide how many phases you want**. I'd suggest eight.

2. **'To eliminate or Not to eliminate** - That is the question.'

You'll likely not want to copy the TV show and take out the slowest team at each checkpoint if you've only got a few teams playing.

Instead, you may have a small prize for the ones who reach a checkpoint first. You may also award points - more for the first . . . less for the last. Those total points would help decide the overall winner.

Another reward you might offer is a shortcut that allows a team to skip over the next challenge, or a detour that one team could play on another that would force them to take on an extra challenge.

If you'd like to do it like the real game and eliminate the slowest team at the checkpoints, you'll need more players. To pull that off, you might want to invite friends and neighbors to participate. With more families playing there can now be more than more than one house involved, you've got more room to spread the course across).

In fact, this approach could be incorporated into a school or neighborhood service project. Wouldn't that would be something for the newspapers!

3. **Map out the course**.

Since most houses don't have the same chore that can be done over and over, most phases of the game should have "first come, first serve" challenge choices.

For example, one phase may be played in the kitchen. The first team to arrive may pick a task that has to do with sweeping the floors, the second picks the task that has something to do with taking out the garbage, and the third team may have to load a pile of dirty dishes.

Pick an area for each phase. So if you picked eight "legs of the race" and your race is just around the house, you may choose, the garage, the backyard, the kitchen, the bathroom, the front yard, the family room, a bedroom, the laundry room.

Then, for each area, pick enough tasks for each team to do. So, if there's three teams - each area needs three tasks.

If you want to give your course an "around the world" feel to it - you might want to put up a sign and a few pictures or items representing each country. It's totally optional.

If your course goes beyond your own property, make sure you explain the **rules** of safety and respect that must be followed at all times (no reckless dashing out into the street, or jumping a neighbor's fence to cut through their backyard, or trampling flower beds and such).

If you're going to travel longer distances, to do chores in several houses or even take on a task like grocery shopping - try to have a car and driver for each team.

If you only have one car - keep track of the times each team got back in the car. Once they've been returned home, they can get out of the car, to continue the race, in the same order with the same time spacing.

You may even want to mix in a local service opportunity or two into your course to really spice things up. (Pull weeds at a local cemetery, wash car windows at a local gas station, mow a widow's lawn - with permission)

4. **Make each challenge interesting.** You're not looking for the most efficient way to get a job done here - you're shooting for the most memorable one.

For example, a task may be to take out the garbage. But to do so, a team may have to pull it off with their hands tied behind their back.

Or what if dishes had to be loaded while wearing oven mitts?

And sweeping the floors could be done with one teammate sitting in a rolling chair with a broom while the other pushed the chair (you could take it up a notch by blindfolding the one pushing while the sitting one has to verbally navigate).

At the end of each task, set up a checkpoint (something simple like a foam mat and a flag). Once a team has checked in and gotten their prizes and points and such, you'll also hand them a clue for the next leg of their "journey."

You can be direct and just give instructions, 'Go to this place.' Or you can give those who are behind a chance to catch up by making the clue more intriguing.

You may hand each team a very close-up picture of part of a lamp post so that they need to figure out what and where it is. Or you may do a math problem that leads to a house number. Players may need to find a particular person and give them a password to receive further instructions.

5. Prepare.

Here's a checklist for the race's Homestyle Edition course:

- 8 checkpoints (could be a flag and foam mat or a place that's simply taped off. Feel free to be creative!). If you're short on supplies - you could also just have one or two checkpoints and just move them from area to area.
- 8 instruction sheets for each team telling them where to go to and for the next "leg of the journey." Could be placed in envelopes.
- 8 signs to label each area as a country. (I think you should always dub the dining room "Hungary." and the kitchen "Cook Islands.") - The Signs optional as are any other exotic **props** you might want to throw in.
- Instructions for each challenge to be posted at the challenge.
- A clipboard with a simple score sheet to keep track of each team's points earned at each checkpoint.
- Small prizes for the winners of each checkpoint.

- A few shortcut, roadblock or detour cards.
- A grand prize for the players who come in first at the last get of the game and/or for the team with the most overall points.
- Any **props** needed for each task.

6. **Cover the Bases**. Make sure you've got enough people to help. You'll need someone to host the checkpoints, explain the challenges, and judge each task. It is possible to have one person do it all, but so much easier if you've got several helpers. Drivers and even a Race photographer are other jobs.

7. Split **up into teams and . . . Go!**

8. **Name a winning team(s) and hand out prizes**. You could do this immediately after the race, or hold a special evening to announce the winners and perhaps even show pictures and video highlights.

Chapter 5: Now What?!

Have you ever tried to cook every recipe in even one of your cookbooks? Wouldn't that be a cross-eyed, head-banging, stomach-churning thing to do?!

A cookbook is simply a resource guide. You glance through it, pick out what fits your needs and what you have to work with. Then you pull together your menu.

In the same spirit, many ideas in this book might be appetizing to you, But trying to take them ALL on at once?! You'd have to be 2 marimbas short of a Mariachi Band want to try that!

And, of course, you don't have to. May I offer a simple strategy that will help you get the most out of this book?

Quick and Easy 8-Step Plan 'o Action!

1. Answer this question - What improvement do you most want to see when it comes to your kids and chores?

- *Is it a better attitude when you need help?*
- *Do you want to see a cleaner bedroom?*
- *Would you like to strengthen your relationships?*
- *Do you want to instill a sense of pride in a job well done?*
- *Want your kids to be self-motivated about cleaning*
- *Trying to help them be more service-oriented?*

The more you see your target, the more likely you are to hit it!

2. Skim through this book and pick the top five activities that will help you make your target dream a reality, Jot them down. Feel free to take those activities and "Beat 'em, bust 'em and re-adjust 'em" to fit your family.

3. Involve your kids. Ask them if they will support you in coming up with more enjoyable ways to tackle chores. Invite their honest feedback and ideas to improve on the activities (short of suggesting you do everything!).

4. Get a baseline - your family's starting place. Go around the house with a camera and capture images of messy rooms, or do shorty-video interviews asking kids how they feel about chores. Could your child do the filming?

5. Commit on your calendar! When will you do each of these 5 activities? You might want to kick in today . . . or build anticipation by doing a countdown. Just make sure to keep it very bite-sized.

6. Go for it!

Try to capture the fun on film.

The time this one takes depends on you!

7. Evaluate your progress. This could be as simple as a 5 minute conversation. You could also check out your "Before

and After" pictures or videos. What did your family like and what could be changed to make it better next time?

8. Repeat the process. Once you've sampled each of the five activities on the "menu," you can do your favorites again. You can also move on to a new target goal and/or a try out 5 new activities.

Want to go beyond the recipes for fun work in this book?

Now that you have access to all the ingredients in the "Pantry of Fun" you're free to come up with your own homemade treats!

Here's a formula you can use to come up with your own recipes:

1. Pick a chore.

2. Choose ingredients from the Pantry of Fun and consider which could be added to that chore. props can be especially helpful - so look around the house for items you can use. Keep in mind your target goal and the lessons your want your kids to learn.

3. Brainstorm creative ways to combine the chore, the ingredient(s) of fun (especially props from around the house). Bring in the "Big Guns!" - Ask your kids for help. Not only can kids be a great source of unbridled ideas - they'll also have a sense of ownership when it comes time to try out their ideas.

Why don't we play with this formula for a minute and watch how it can help you cook up your own family favorites?!

I'm going to play a mom who has a target goal and a family of 3 children - ages 4 to 8. (You might even want to cover each step to see what you can come up with before you read what I've written . . .). Here we go! . . .

Target Goal:

"Help siblings develop a closer relationship"

1. **Pick a chore:**

   Let's see what we can do with "Pulling weeds in the yard."

Choose ingredients.

I want this recipe tailored to my target goal. It needs to work for my family's ages, interests, resources and such, so I'm going to pull out . . .

IMAGINATION - Goes great on everything!

CHALLENGE - Since I'm going for more team spirit in the family, I won't be doing a competition that will have the kids at odds with each other. Think I'll do something where the kids need to cooperate to beat a time deadline.

RULES - This is a simple task with young kids, so I want the rules short and sweet.

EXCITEMENT - An "Easy going" pace won't work here if I'm doing a time limit, so I want to do something that's going to get the kids "fired up" and itching to go! Music can really help as can a good story-line.

PROPS - Looking around the house, I find:

- A laundry basket
- Some rope
- A towel
- A toy fire-fighter's helmet
- A garden hose
- The backyard deck
- A bucket.

SOCIALIZATION - Since the goal is to help build relationships, I need something cooperative.

2. **Brainstorm** ideas for each ingredient.

Let's start with "Imagination."

- I'm going to pretend the weeds are something else. Could be . . . landmines . . . wild animals ("Dandy Lions?!!! :o) . . . trapped people . . . food supplies . . . medicine . . .
- I'd like the kids to feel like they're part of a heroic team with a big job to do. I'm thinking along the lines of Rescue Heroes . . . Super Friends . . . The Backyardigans . . .
- They'll need a rescue scene.
- Ones that come to mind: Marooned on an island . . . sick people needing supplies . . . a Tsunami coming . . . freeing trapped people surrounded by landmines left by a villain . . . being chased by the IRS . .
- Now, I'll boil down the scene by just picking from my list of choices with the help of my kids.

Together, we come up with "**imagination**" looking like this:

Bad news!
A Tsunami is coming this way!
.. and there's a village in its path!

We are Rescue Heroes
who need to get in
and evacuate everyone we can
. . . very, very quickly . . .

Next, I'll mix in the challenge of a time-limit.

I'd like the kids to work about 15 minutes and can use an egg timer to sound the alarm when the Tsunami hits - or - I can use the bucket and garden hose.

I could set the hose to drip slowly into the bucket and say that when the bucket overflows, the Tsunami has hit. I could then turn the hose on full blast and spray the yard (and everyone in it) to simulate the Tsunami.

The simple **rules** I picked to set up this challenge are:

You must get as many people (weeds)
as you can to safety
before the bucket overflows
and water hits the village.

Now, here's how I'll use those **props**. I need a place for the kids to put the weeds - I mean - rescue the villagers. I've got the laundry basket. I've also got rope that I can tie to that basket to pull it to safety.

I could throw in music, for **excitement** but our neighbor works the night shift, so turning up music this time is out.

Instead, we'll use a lot of urgency in our voices to alert each other in stifled whispers whenever another villager (weed) is spotted.

We could throw in "whooshing" noises to help imagine a bad storm.

So **excitement** and **props** combine like this:

We need you to help as many
passengers as you can
into the helicopter (laundry basket)
to airlift them to safety
(Hoist the weeds from ground level
to the top of the deck)
. . . before the Tsunami hits.
Any weed - er - anyone . . .
left behind could be lost at sea.

Now. this may sound like a lot, but let's step back and see what it would take to pull this adventure off:

1. Set out your **props**. Tie a rope to a laundry basket and throw the other end up to your deck. Put a garden hose in a bucket of water and turn it on just a bit.
2. Briefly explain their mission.
3. Go!

Hopefully, walking through this "formula for fun" will help you as you concoct on your own recipes to turn work into great memories!

Please feel free to show and tell your great ideas online with the rest of us! I'll be revising this book and will be including the best ideas from our online community - giving credit where credit is due and with your permission, of course!

Chapter 6: The Next Level

At this point, hopefully you're very sad . . . that you've come to the end of this book.

But, it doesn't have to end!

Parenting is a team sport! If you haven't done it already - why not join us online?!

Our site: www.Cleaning-Games.com is a place for parents and kids to share what works and what could work better. You'll also find helpful resources there from charts and badges to recommendations. Watch for contests and prizes to boot!

It's tied to our FaceBook page too, so you'll have plenty of opportunity to socialize with friendly folk!

If you haven't picked it up already, you can get a free copy of my eBook, "**How To Bring Tantrums and Fighting To A Screeching Halt**" with 10 out-of-the-box, fun ideas.

You'll not only get the book, but you'll also get a membership to "The Parents' Toolbox" (Free for now - as of this October 2013 edition) where I'll not only email you more cleaning fun stuff – but also other helpful resources related to helping you raise your children in the spirit of a great adventure!

Watch for goodies like

- How to make "Magic Milk"
- Where to go for a free, high-quality game that has even the youngest kids learning multiplication, division, etc.
- How to involve your kids in volunteer work and greatly simplify the sign-up process with your school
- Go on a learning adventure with printable "secret codes" that can be deciphered with your smart phone.
- How to make GIANT soap bubbles (as high as you!)

If you're subscribed to "The Parents' Toolbox," you can get free copies of my books during special launch promotions. Look for more creative ideas, short stories, contests, news and whatever goodies I can think of to send your way!

In the Future . . .

Watch for a whole series of adventure comic books for kids. It'll be interactive "edu-tainment" that will help them learn life skills (manners, citizenship, safety, emergency prep . . . the works!) in a playful, humorous way.

I'll also be introducing a new comic-book series about exciting true heroes to inspire our rising generation.

I've also got at least one app for your mobile device coming that will make "Bomb Squad" and other games even more entertaining. I'll let you know when that's out. Just watch for it on the website and in "The Parents' Toolbox" newsletter.

Also – This "Begging" book is just a first phase. The goal of Adventure Aisle is to help kids and families unplug and have real adventures, so my next parenting book will be about how to create "Magic from the Mundane."

This book has evolved from well-received workshops where I've shared how to take snore-inducing, common, everyday things and turn them into adventures where you'll have more fun than a couple of foxes in a hen house.

It'll be chuck-full of ideas you've likely never heard before that will help families really treasure each other, discover fun in service, experience "learning in disguise" and help you come up with your own creative FUN-derful ideas! (Yeah - you can do it!)

The activities will appeal to the whole range of ages found in just about any family - from pre-toddler to kids in grown up people's skins to the "chronologically gifted." There will be stories, hopefully something you can call humor, tools and an easy-to-follow plan of action. And it'll all be wrapped up in a swashbuckling adventure theme.

I'll be looking for your help as I put this next book together and will be giving credit and prizes to the best ideas that come from you readers.

These things are only a second phase of a host of fun "shhhhtuff" in the pipeline - all in the spirit of bringing real adventures to our kids and families! So, stay tuned!

One final request!

Did you catch a type-o or formatting goof?! Got any constructive criticism? Do you have any ideas that would help this to be a better book?

I'd love to hear it! It'll help make this a better book!

Please email me directly at Shannon@Cleaning-Games.com.

AND - if you thought this book was helpful, one of the nicest things you could do is put in the good word (even a sentence or two is great!) for this book with Amazon. It'll help others know if you feel it's worth the investment for their own families.

If you're up for it, here's the link:

www.cleaning-games.com/Amazon

And finally – High 5's to you!

You just made it to the end . . . which is just the beginning.

"See" you soon!

Shannon

RECOMMENDED READS

"Cleaning House: A Mom's Twelve-Month Experiment to Rid Her Home of Youth Entitlement" by Kay Wills Wyma.

"For parents who are weary of the Me generation, [Cleaning House] provides a practical roadmap...to bring your children from entitlement to empowerment. From the day-to-day aspects of training in practical-life skills to issues of the heart such as service with a smile and hospitality, Kay writes with transparency, humor, and wisdom. As a parent, grandparent, and school principal, I believe this book will become a favorite of parents and one they will reference frequently." —Jody Capehart, co-author of Bonding with Your Teens Through Boundaries

"How to Talk So Kids Will Listen & Listen So Kids Will Talk" by Adele Faber and Elaine Mazlish

"#1 New York Times bestselling and award-winning authors whose books have sold more than three million copies and have been translated into over thirty languages. How to Talk So Kids Can Learn—At Home and in School, was cited by Child Magazine as the "best book of the year for excellence in family issues in education." The authors' group workshop programs and videos produced by PBS are currently being used by parent and teacher groups around the world"

"Living Clutter-Free with Kids in the House" by Mike Burns

"Mike Burns provides insights into not just de-cluttering, but rethinking about the why of clutter, how it gets there, and the effect this has on families. Finally, he provides practical tips for including children in the de-cluttering process, and even makes it fun!" - Mara

"Clutter's Last Stand" by Don Aslett

"This book forever changed the way I look at possessions. I tend to be a packrat, but after reading this book I was able to "let go" of a lot of junk and take loads of boxes to Goodwill, take other stuff to the dump, etc. Don Aslett is a very humorous and entertaining writer. His books are among my all-time favorites! I feel "lighter" in every way when my possessions are pared down. I reread this book every year or two to recharge and unload!" - Jeanette

Picture Attributions

Crown: Information |Description={{en|1=Heraldic Crown of Spanish "Señor" (Lord)}} {{es|1=Representación heráldica de la corona española del título de Señor.}} |Source={{own}} |Author=Heralder |Date= |Permission={{own}} |other_versions=[

Cave opening: Image credit: <a href='http://www.123rf.com/photo_13091492_entrance-to-the-cueva-del-viento-of-guajataca-forest-reserve--puerto-rico.html'>wirepec / 123RF Stock Photo</a>

Barbary Apes Sign: fuzuoko on flickr.com fuzuoko's photostream

Barbary Ape Face: http://en.wikipedia.org/wiki/File:Gibraltar_Barbary_Macaque.jpg

Penalty Graphic: Image credit: <a href='http://www.123rf.com/photo_15405053_a-man-is-blowing-the-whistle-warning-someone.html'>abluecup / 123RF Stock Photo</a>

Beach digging: Image credit: <a href='http://www.123rf.com/photo_7263276_children-s-beach-toys--buckets-spade-and-shovel-on-sand-on-a-sunny-day.html'>antartis / 123RF Stock Photo</a>

Station Wagon:
http://commons.wikimedia.org/wiki/File:Innocenti_Elba_station_wagon.jpg

Miniature Garden:
http://commons.wikimedia.org/wiki/File:Miniature_garden,_Drumin_-_geograph.org.uk_-_259173.jpg

Zorbing: http://en.wikipedia.org/wiki/File:Zorbing.jpg

Vortex: http://www.kozzi.com/stock-photo-24788674-abstract-background.html?tag=22719&tags=22719

Eavesdropping Neighbor: http://www.123rf.com/photo_3820900_a-male-office-worker-peers-over-a-cubicle-because-he-is-nosey.html

Checklist: http://www.kozzi.com/stock-clipart-24751540-vector-image-of-a-checklist..html?tag=13810&tags=13810

World Flags: http://www.kozzi.com/stock-clipart-24818102-flaggen_kugel.html?tag=15970&tags=15970,1860

5 Minutes: http://www.123rf.com/photo_4803742_illustration-of-timer.html

15 Minutes: http://www.123rf.com/photo_4803738_illustration-of-timer.html

30 Minutes: http://www.123rf.com/photo_4803741_illustration-of-timer.html

Weeds: http://www.kozzi.com/stock-photo-24809069-dandelions-on-blue-sky-background.html?tag=239&tags=239,9411

Tantrum: http://www.123rf.com/photo_12150342_shouting-angry-asian-kid-on-red-background.html

Flying Dutchman: http://www.123rf.com/photo_6203187_flying-dutchman--sailing-ship.html

Wing Suit: http://en.wikipedia.org/wiki/File:Wingsuit-01.jpg

Made in the USA
San Bernardino, CA
15 May 2014